Lecture Notes in Computer Science   12989

More information about this subseries at https://link.springer.com/bookseries/7409

Kejiang Ye · Liang-Jie Zhang (Eds.)

Cloud Computing – CLOUD 2021

14th International Conference
Held as Part of the Services Conference Federation, SCF 2021
Virtual Event, December 10–14, 2021
Proceedings

 Springer

Editors
Kejiang Ye
Shenzhen Institutes of Advanced Technology,
Chinese Academy of Sciences
Shenzhen, China

Liang-Jie Zhang ⓘ
Kingdee International Software Group
Co., Ltd.
Shenzhen, China

ISSN 0302-9743   ISSN 1611-3349 (electronic)
Lecture Notes in Computer Science
ISBN 978-3-030-96325-5   ISBN 978-3-030-96326-2 (eBook)
https://doi.org/10.1007/978-3-030-96326-2

LNCS Sublibrary: SL3 – Information Systems and Applications, incl. Internet/Web, and HCI

Preface

The International Conference on Cloud Computing (CLOUD) is a prime international forum for both researchers and industry practitioners to exchange the latest fundamental advances in the state of the art and practice of cloud computing, identify emerging research topics, and define the future of cloud computing. All topics regarding cloud computing align with the theme of CLOUD.

CLOUD is a member of the Services Conference Federation (SCF). SCF 2021 comprised the following 10 collocated service-oriented sister conferences: the International Conference on Web Services (ICWS 2021), the International Conference on Cloud Computing (CLOUD 2021), the International Conference on Services Computing (SCC 2021), the International Conference on Big Data (BigData 2021), the International Conference on AI and Mobile Services (AIMS 2021), the World Congress on Services (SERVICES 2021), the International Conference on Internet of Things (ICIOT 2021), the International Conference on Cognitive Computing (ICCC 2021), the International Conference on Edge Computing (EDGE 2021), and the International Conference on Blockchain (ICBC 2021).

This volume presents the accepted papers for CLOUD 2021, held virtually over the Internet during December 10–14, 2021. For this conference, each paper was reviewed by three independent members of the international Program Committee. After carefully evaluating their originality and quality, seven papers were accepted.

We are pleased to thank the authors whose submissions and participation made this conference possible. We also want to express our thanks to the Program Committee members for their dedication in helping to organize the conference and reviewing the submissions.

Finally, we would like to thank operation committee members Sheng He and Yishuang Ning for their excellent work in organizing this conference. We look forward to your future contributions as volunteers, authors, and conference participants in the fast-growing worldwide services innovations community.

December 2021

Kejiang Ye
Liang-Jie Zhang

Organization

CLOUD 2021 Program Chair

Kejiang Ye   Shenzhen Institutes of Advanced Technology,
                                    Chinese Academy of Sciences, China

Services Conference Federation (SCF 2021)

General Chairs

Wu Chou   Essenlix Corporation, USA
Calton Pu (Co-chair)   Georgia Tech, USA
Dimitrios Georgakopoulos   Swinburne University of Technology, Australia

Program Chairs

Liang-Jie Zhang   Kingdee International Software Group Co., Ltd.,
                                    China
Ali Arsanjani   Amazon Web Services, USA

CFO

Min Luo   Georgia Tech, USA

Industry Track Chairs

Awel Dico   Etihad Airways, UAE
Rajesh Subramanyan   Amazon Web Services, USA
Siva Kantamneni   Deloitte Consulting, USA

Industry Exhibit and International Affairs Chair

Zhixiong Chen   Mercy College, USA

Operation Committee

Jing Zeng   China Gridcom Co., Ltd., China
Yishuang Ning   Tsinghua University, China
Sheng He   Tsinghua University, China

Steering Committee

Calton Pu (Co-chair)	Georgia Tech, USA
Liang-Jie Zhang (Co-chair)	Kingdee International Software Group Co., Ltd., China

CLOUD 2021 Program Committee

Gerald Baumgartner	Louisiana State University, USA
Feng Chen	Louisiana State University, USA
Haopeng Chen	Shanghai Jiao Tong University, China
Jingshu Chen	Oakland University, USA
Dazhao Cheng	University of North Carolina at Charlotte, USA
A. Daniel	MMMUT, India
Shahram Ghandeharizadeh	University of Southern California, USA
Yasuhiko Kanemasa	Fujitsu Laboratories Ltd., Japan
Hidehiro Kanemitsu	Tokyo University of Technology, Japan
Krishna Kant	Temple University, USA
Yao Liu	Rutgers University, USA
Supratik Mukhopadhyay	Louisiana State University, USA
Nagendra Kumar Nainar	CISCO, USA
Mara Nikolaidou	Harokopio University of Athens, Greece
Li Pan	Shandong University, China
Sanjay Patel	KSV, India
Rkn Sai Krishna	Teradata India Pvt Ltd, India
Ruediger Schulze	IBM Germany Research and Development GmbH, Germany
Huasong Shan	JD.com, Inc., USA
Jun Shen	University of Wollongong, Australia
Byung Chul Tak	Kyungpook National University, South Korea
Anand Tripathi	University of Minnesota, USA
Nan Wang	Heilongjiang University, China
Wei Wang	University of Texas at San Antonio, USA
Yingwei Wang	University of Prince Edward Island, Canada
Yuehua Wang	Texas A & M University-Commerce, USA
Pengcheng Xiong	Amazon, USA
Hailu Xu	California State University, USA
Feng Yan	University of Nevada, Reno, USA
Ming Zhao	Arizona State University, USA

Conference Sponsor – Services Society

The Services Society (S2) is a non-profit professional organization that has been created to promote worldwide research and technical collaboration in services innovations among academia and industrial professionals. Its members are volunteers from industry and academia with common interests. S2 is registered in the USA as a "501(c) organization", which means that it is an American tax-exempt non-profit organization. S2 collaborates with other professional organizations to sponsor or co-sponsor conferences and to promote an effective services curriculum in colleges and universities. S2 initiates and promotes a "Services University" program worldwide to bridge the gap between industrial needs and university instruction.

The services sector accounted for 79.5% of the GDP of the USA in 2016. Hong Kong has one of the world's most service-oriented economies, with the services sector accounting for more than 90% of GDP. As such, the Services Society has formed 10 Special Interest Groups (SIGs) to support technology and domain specific professional activities:

- Special Interest Group on Web Services (SIG-WS)
- Special Interest Group on Services Computing (SIG-SC)
- Special Interest Group on Services Industry (SIG-SI)
- Special Interest Group on Big Data (SIG-BD)
- Special Interest Group on Cloud Computing (SIG-CLOUD)
- Special Interest Group on Artificial Intelligence (SIG-AI)
- Special Interest Group on Edge Computing (SIG-EC)
- Special Interest Group on Cognitive Computing (SIG-CC)
- Special Interest Group on Blockchain (SIG-BC)
- Special Interest Group on Internet of Things (SIG-IOT)

About the Services Conference Federation (SCF)

As the founding member of the Services Conference Federation (SCF), the First International Conference on Web Services (ICWS) was held in June 2003 in Las Vegas, USA. A sister event, the First International Conference on Web Services - Europe 2003 (ICWS-Europe 2003) was held in Germany in October of the same year. In 2004, ICWS-Europe was changed to the European Conference on Web Services (ECOWS), which was held in Erfurt, Germany. The 19th edition in the conference series, SCF 2021, was held virtually over the Internet during December 10–14, 2021.

In the past 18 years, the ICWS community has expanded from Web engineering innovations to scientific research for the whole services industry. The service delivery platforms have expanded to mobile platforms, the Internet of Things (IoT), cloud computing, and edge computing. The services ecosystem has gradually been enabled, value added, and intelligence embedded through enabling technologies such as big data, artificial intelligence, and cognitive computing. In the coming years, transactions with multiple parties involved will by transformed blockchain.

Based on the technology trends and best practices in the field, SCF will continue serving as the conference umbrella's code name for all services-related conferences. SCF 2021 defined the future of the New ABCDE (AI, Blockchain, Cloud, big Data, Everything is connected), which enable IOT and support the "5G for Services Era". SCF 2021 featured 10 colocated conferences all centered around the topic of "services", each focusing on exploring different themes (e.g. web-based services, cloud-based services, big data-based services, services innovation lifecycle, AI-driven ubiquitous services, blockchain-driven trust service-ecosystems, industry-specific services and applications, and emerging service-oriented technologies). The SCF 2021 members were as follows:

1. The 2021 International Conference on Web Services (ICWS 2021, http://icws.org/), which was the flagship conference for web-based services featuring web services modeling, development, publishing, discovery, composition, testing, adaptation, and delivery, as well as the latest API standards.
2. The 2021 International Conference on Cloud Computing (CLOUD 2021, http://the cloudcomputing.org/), which was the flagship conference for modeling, developing, publishing, monitoring, managing, and delivering XaaS (everything as a service) in the context of various types of cloud environments.
3. The 2021 International Conference on Big Data (BigData 2021, http://bigdataco ngress.org/), which focused on the scientific and engineering innovations of big data.
4. The 2021 International Conference on Services Computing (SCC 2021, http://the scc.org/), which was the flagship conference for the services innovation lifecycle including enterprise modeling, business consulting, solution creation, services orchestration, services optimization, services management, services marketing, and business process integration and management.

5. The 2021 International Conference on AI and Mobile Services (AIMS 2021, http://ai1000.org/), which addressed the science and technology of artificial intelligence and the development, publication, discovery, orchestration, invocation, testing, delivery, and certification of AI-enabled services and mobile applications.
6. The 2021 World Congress on Services (SERVICES 2021, http://servicescongress.org/), which put its focus on emerging service-oriented technologies and industry-specific services and solutions.
7. The 2021 International Conference on Cognitive Computing (ICCC 2021, http://thecognitivecomputing.org/), which put its focus on Sensing Intelligence (SI) as a Service (SIaaS), making a system listen, speak, see, smell, taste, understand, interact, and/or walk, in the context of scientific research and engineering solutions.
8. The 2021 International Conference on Internet of Things (ICIOT 2021, http://iciot.org/), which addressed the creation of IoT technologies and the development of IOT services.
9. The 2021 International Conference on Edge Computing (EDGE 2021, http://theedgecomputing.org/), which put its focus on the state of the art and practice of edge computing including, but not limited to, localized resource sharing, connections with the cloud, and 5G devices and applications.
10. The 2021 International Conference on Blockchain (ICBC 2021, http://blockchain1000.org/), which concentrated on blockchain-based services and enabling technologies.

Some of the highlights of SCF 2021 were as follows:

- Bigger Platform: The 10 collocated conferences (SCF 2021) got sponsorship from the Services Society which is the world-leading not-for-profits organization (501 c(3)) dedicated to serving more than 30,000 services computing researchers and practitioners worldwide. A bigger platform means bigger opportunities for all volunteers, authors, and participants. In addition, Springer provided sponsorship for best paper awards and other professional activities. All 10 conference proceedings of SCF 2021 will be published by Springer and indexed in the ISI Conference Proceedings Citation Index (included in Web of Science), the Engineering Index EI (Compendex and Inspec databases), DBLP, Google Scholar, IO-Port, MathSciNet, Scopus, and ZBlMath.
- Brighter Future: While celebrating the 2021 version of ICWS, SCF 2021 highlighted the Fourth International Conference on Blockchain (ICBC 2021) to build the fundamental infrastructure for enabling secure and trusted services ecosystems. It will also lead our community members to create their own brighter future.
- Better Model: SCF 2021 continued to leverage the invented Conference Blockchain Model (CBM) to innovate the organizing practices for all 10 collocated conferences.

Contents

A Brokering Model for the Cloud Market

Georgios Chatzithanasis(✉) ⓘ, Evangelia Filiopoulou ⓘ,
Christos Michalakelis ⓘ, and Mara Nikolaidou ⓘ

Department of Informatics and Telematics, Harokopio University,
Omirou 9 PS, 17778 Athens, Greece
geo.hatz@hua.gr
https://dit.hua.gr

Abstract. The cloud broker is an IT role and a business model that
acts as an intermediary agent between cloud providers and end users. The
exponentially increasing adoption of the IaaS market has contributed significantly to the so far growth of the Cloud Broker market. The unprecedented scenario of COVID-19 pandemic has upgraded the role and the
contribution of broker to the cloud market, since cloud adoption has
been further accelerated by the COVID-19 crisis. Cloud broker guaran-
tees the availability of a given amount of resources for use at a specific
time, offering pricing policies that benefit consumers and boost broker's
profitability. Into that context a cloud brokering model, is introduced and
described, together with a profit maximization economic model, suggesting and evaluating different pricing policies that ensure the viability of
the business and boost profitability. The pricing policy that is able to
lead to the maximum profit potential is also highlighted.

Keywords: Brokering model · Pricing · Cloud computing

1 Introduction

The Infrastructure-as-a-Service (IaaS) market has been on growth for several
years and there are no indications leading to a lowering of demand in the foreseeable future [27]. In addition, the rapid global spread of COVID-19 has forced
almost all sector of financial market, such as small and large businesses, health-
care and education to digitally transform. Therefore, the COVID-19 impact on
cloud computing is tremendous and IaaS market is highly affected [1,20].

The increasing adoption of IaaS market has contributed significantly to the
growth of the cloud broker market which is expected to register a CAGR of 16.6%
until 2024 [25]. Moreover, the unprecedented scenario of COVID-19 pandemic
has upgraded the role and the contribution of broker to the cloud market, since
cloud adoption has been further accelerated by the COVID-19 outbreak.

Cloud broker is an IT role and business model and acts as an intermediary
between cloud providers and end users [21]. It combines and integrates multiple
services into one or more new services and enhances a given service by improving

K. Ye and L.-J. Zhang (Eds.): CLOUD 2021, LNCS 12989, pp. 1–16, 2022.
https://doi.org/10.1007/978-3-030-96326-2_1

some specific capability and providing value-added services to cloud consumers. Finally, the cloud broker, aims to attract consumers and increase the market share, offering higher discounts than cloud providers, reducing the cost for cloud users [9].

The cloud broker business model , is built upon ensuring economic viability and profitability, based on a proper pricing policy. The price of a service affects consumer demand and this in return affects the revenues generated by the firm [1].

Into that context a Brokering model is described and analysed. Broker initially reserves instances (VMs) from cloud providers for a specific time period, gaining a significant discount. The discount is related to the reservation time, therefore broker chooses a reservation period, combined with a price that fits the capital budget. Thence, broker leases the VMs to end-users, at a price lower than the on-demand provider's price, in order to attract more users and increase the market share. In the context of this work, a profit maximization economic model is proposed, suggesting and evaluating different pricing policies that ensure the viability of the business and boost profitability. The pricing policy that leads to the maximum profit potential is also analysed.

Broker's pricing policies are related to the corresponding policies of the providers, since they both claim a share in the cloud market. Cloud providers adopt different pricing policies under different commitment terms. The most popular is the "pay-as-you-go" pricing, referring to "on-demand" instances where users pay a fixed price for virtual machines (VMs) per billing cycle without any commitment [13]. In addition, the subscription-based policy is used for Reserved Instances (RI), where users pay a onetime upfront fee for a time period, as for example a monthly subscription.

The economic model proposes pricing policies based on cloud providers pricing schemes. The on-demand pricing is used as a reference point for the evaluation of the model. For the development of the pricing policy the price evolution over a specific time period is taken into account. This concept is rather challenging and innovative, since profit analysis is usually linked to the consumer demand for the given product or service.

The importance of the proposed methodology, which constitutes the contributions to the corresponding literature can be summarised to the following topics:

- Broker set the prices of the resources based on the prices set by cloud providers.
- The financial viability of the investment is examined.
- The profit potential of each proposed pricing policy is highlighted.
- The social surplus, in terms of the end-users and broker's surplus is estimated.

The rest of the paper is organized as follows: Sect. 2 presents the related work, while Sect. 3 describes the cloud pricing and introduces the proposed profit maximization model. Section 4 presents a case study of the model for the evaluation of the model. Finally Sect. 5 concludes the paper and suggests future work.

2 Related Work

There are several papers available in the relevant literature that discuss the cloud broker business model, including studies that address the broker's profit maximization.

In [22] a different kind of broker was introduced, relying on outsourcing virtual machines (VMs) to customers. Virtual Machine Planning Problem was defined that tried to address broker's profit maximization. In addition, a number of efficient smart heuristics was proposed, aiming to allocate a set of VM requests from customers into the available pre-booked ones, that maximized the broker earnings. In [26] the authors introduced two algorithms that maximize the profit of the cloud broker. Dynamic pricing was adopted to adjust users demand under Quantized Billing Cycles. In [29] a fair and priority aware pricing scheme was designed, known as Priority Pricing, aiming to address the idle resource waste.

In [28] a profit maximization problem was modeled based on optimal multi-server configuration and VM pricing. Finally, a heuristic method was introduced to address the optimization problem. In [21] the cloud broker was introduced as a novel business role between cloud providers and cloud users and was described by a multiserver, a revenue and a cost model. In addition users' demand holds a determinant role in the broker's profit maximization problem.

It is evident that the profit maximization models of the review are strongly related to consumer demand. A different approach is presented to the present paper, based on the evolution of cloud pricing through time, aiming to fill the identified gap in the relevant literature. Amazon's pricing policy was adopted for the evaluation of the model which, according to literature, follows an important annual reduction in the on-demand price [19].

3 Problem Statement

3.1 Cloud Market Pricing

Many companies offer Cloud Computing options and have facilitate the everyday life of IT departments but also have proven highly cost effective. The leaders in the market are the Amazon Web Services (AWS) [2], Microsoft Azure [5], IBM, and Google [23]. These providers represent the 55% of the cloud infrastructure services market, in total [3].

One of the major features of cloud computing follows the "pay-as-you-go" pricing model, where the user pays according to the amount of resources consumed [7]. However, the "pay-as-you-go" model is complex as it requires continuous monitoring of resource usage [31].

In addition, the majority of cloud providers offer two pricing schemes: the on-demand and the reserved instances. The former enable users to pay per hour computing capacity with no long-term commitments. Reserved instances (RI) pricing schemes offer users the option to reserve Virtual Machines (VMs) for a specific time period, for example one year. RI are not physical instances but rather a discount billing concept in which user purchases VMs for a fixed time period and in return providers offer significant discounts, as compared to the equivalent on-demand instances price. The amount of the discount varies according to the length of the commitment and the available payment options. It is evident that reserved instances are cost-effective if workloads are steady, whereas on-demand instances are considered to be a more suitable solution when the workload rate is scattered. The broker of the current paper interacts with providers and purchases reserved instances and leases them to users, aiming to be profitable. Profit making is among its main objectives, hence, the following section examines a broker's profit maximization problem.

3.2 Proposed Profit Maximization Model

IaaS providers usually offer resources for varying periods of time, either on demand, i.e. for a short period of time, or for a longer period. Amazon [2], for example, apart from the on-demand supply offers IaaS for a maximum period of three years. The pricing scheme is based on the assumption that the price of IaaS is reversely proportional to the reservation time. This means that the longer the time infrastructure is reserved, the lower the reservation price for the resource.

Broker has a strong incentive to reserve resources for a long time, as this can contribute to the maximization of the profit, based on the proposed methodology. Therefore, broker is assumed to reserve a quantity of infrastructure from an IaaS provider for a long period of time. Into that time frame, which constitutes the period the corresponding investment is valuated, the broker creates bundles and offers them into the marketplace for a shorter period of time, at a higher price than the price they were reserved; but definitely lower than the current on-demand price of the provider, during each period of time. It is assumed that broker will lease instances to users continuously and the resources will not be idle. In addition, the difference between the reservation price and the selling price drives the creation of the broker's revenues and the consequent profit. Figure 1 illustrates the broker model.

The above assumptions can be mathematically formulated as follows:

At the beginning of the period under evaluation, t_0, broker reserves a quantity, Q, of virtual machines, at a price of $P_{res}(t)$ per unit, for a time period t^*, at a total cost C, as presented in Eq. 1.

$$C = P_{res}(t) * Q \tag{1}$$

The function $P_{res}(t)$ denotes the price that the broker pays to the provider for reserving VMs for t period of time. Without loss of generality, it can be assumed that $P_{res}(t)$ is linear:

$$P_{res}(t) = \beta t + P_{res_0} \ , \ \beta < 0 \tag{2}$$

where P_{res_0} is the price of the reserved VMs for the minimum possible time period and the coefficient β describes the price decrease due to discount derived from the provider's pricing policy.

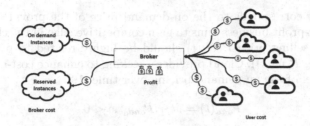

Fig. 1. Cloud broker overview

Following that, broker creates time-based bundles, Q_i, of these VMs and supplies the retail market. Each bundle, Q_i, is then reserved for time t_i at a price of $P_{sell,j}$ creating a revenue R as presented in Eq. 3

$$R_i = Q_i * P_{sell,j} \tag{3}$$

The selling price $P_{sell,j}$ is reduced over time, as technology evolves and new cloud instances are introduced. The function $Psell(t)$ denotes the price reduction of the VMs for a specific time period.

$$P_{sell}(t) = \gamma t + P_{sell_0} \,,\, \gamma < 0 \tag{4}$$

where P_{sell_0} is the maximum price that broker sells to users an amount of VMs for the minimum reservation time and the coefficient γ denotes the price decrease due to the introduction of new cloud solutions.

Thus, the total revenue deriving by the total quantity Q is depicted in Eq. 5.

$$R = \sum_{i=1}^{n} R_i = \sum_{i-1}^{n} Q_i * P_{sell,j} \tag{5}$$

In the context of this analysis, it can be assumed that the market demand for cloud resources will cover the total reserved quantity, Q. This is a quite valid assumption, since cloud services merit a continuously increasing demand and it can be also verified by performing a forecasting analysis regarding the demand for the time period t^*. The total profit, P, for the broker model is given by the following Eq. 6.

$$P = R - C = \sum_{i=1}^{n} R_i - P_{res} * Q = \sum_{i-1}^{n} Q_i * P_{sell,j} - P_{res} * Q \tag{6}$$

which, in turn, corresponds to the maximization of P, within the time period under consideration, t^*.

$$\left.\begin{array}{l} \max P = \max\left(R - C\right) = \max(\sum_{i=1}^{n} R_i - P_{res} * Q) \\ \max P = \max(\sum_{i-1}^{n} Q_i * P_{sell,j} - P_{res} * Q) \\ \text{subject to: } P_{res} < P_{sell,j} < P_{ond}(t) \end{array}\right\} \text{M1}$$

where P_{ond} corresponds to the on-demand price of the provider, at time t. Broker as a for-profit business aims to gain competitive edge in the cloud market therefore, the selling price $Psell(t)$ should be highly related to provider's on-demand pricing $P_ond(t)$). Cloud providers, seeking to enhance cost-effectiveness, reduce the level of the on-demand pricing over time [19].

$$P_{ond}(t) = \delta t + P_{ond_0} , \delta < 0 \tag{7}$$

Following the above statement, $P_{sell,j}$ can be expressed as a function of $P_{ond}(t)$:

$$P_{sell,j} = f(P_{ond}(t)) \tag{8}$$

Function f apart from the value of $P_{ond}(t)$ accommodates other marketing variables as well, such as competition, broker's brand name and market reputation, as well as other parameters that define the range within which broker can set $P_{sell,j}$. This function reflects the elasticity of $P_{sell,j}$ in response to $P_{ond}(t)$. In a simpler approach and without loss of generality, if the market factors are considered constant during the evaluation time, $P_{sell,j}$ can be expressed as constantly proportional to $P_{ond}(t)$ by a factor α.

$$P_{sell,j} = \alpha * P_{ond}(t), a \leq 1 \tag{9}$$

The inequality $\alpha \leq 1$ indicates that broker is expected to supply the resources at a lower price than the provider's on-demand price, at each time, since if this does not hold the end user would prefer to obtain resources directly by the provider itself. The value of α, in this case as well, depends on the same factors, including brand name, competition and market concentration and other specific marketing mix variables.

As far as the pricing policy is considered and based on the above analysis, the pricing strategy of broker, i.e. the level of $P_{sell,j}$ depends on a number of parameters that describe the market environment, like competition and market reputation of the broker. If no competitor exists, broker can follow a cost-based pricing approach, by placing a price cap or a price margin over the Pres. However, if other brokers operate in the market, corresponding pricing strategies should be adopted to accommodate this fact. In each case the market reputation and the brand name of the broker determines the level of P_{res} as they strongly related to the confidence of the retail market to the broker and drive their decision to reserve their IaaS from broker or from the original provider, even at a higher price. For example, a well-established broker can set a higher price, closer to the $P_{ond}(t)$ than a newcomer, or a not well-established one.

The following figure illustrates the proposed model.

Figure 2 illustrates broker's two-fold interaction with the providers and users. Initially, broker reserves instances for time t_{res} at a price $P_{res}(t)$. Therefore area C corresponds to the cost that broker pays to the provider for RIs. RIs are a discount billing concept in which broker purchases VMs for a fixed time period and in return providers offer significant discount. The aforementioned Eq. 1 is depicted in Fig. 2 and describes the evolution of the reservation price, thus the

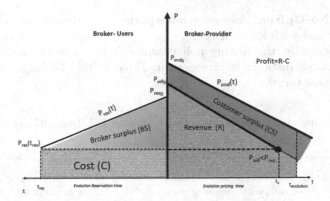

Fig. 2. Profit maximization model

area BS defines the broker surplus. Broker surplus is the monetary gain obtained by broker because resources can be purchased at a lower price according to reservation time [6].

In addition, broker leases the VMs to consumers at price $P_{sell}(t)$ and, aiming to be competitive, the selling price is lower than the on-demand price $P_{ond}(t)$ of the providers. Figure 2 also presents the evolution of the selling and on-demand pricing based on the Eqs. 4 and 7 respectively over time $t_{evolution}$, where $t_{evolution} = t_{res}$. Hence, area CS describes customer surplus, that is the monetary gain obtained by consumers because broker offers them resources at a lower price than the provider [6], whereas area R displays broker's revenue. Broker's profit equals to the difference between R area and cost area C. Finally, when the broker has gained a considerable profit, hypothetically at the t_s the selling price can be lower than the corresponding reservation price.

4 Case Study

4.1 Amazon Web Services-AWS

Numerous cloud providers offer various solutions, however Amazon [2] still remains the leader and has established to hold the largest market share of the cloud market [27] for several years. Amazon offers reserved and on-demand instances. On-demand instances are charged on a per-hour or per-second (minimum 60 s) basis with no long-term commitment. Instead, reserved instances are offered with a significant discount (up to 75%), as compared to on-demand pricing. By using reserved capacity, businesses can minimize risks, more predictably manage budgets and comply with policies that require longer-term commitments [14,15]. In addition, Amazon's users can also choose three different RI payment options [4]: In **Full-Upfront** users need to pay in advance the total cost of the RI, but offers the largest discount. With **Partial-Upfront** users pay 50% in advance with an additional monthly cost and get lower discount compared to full-upfront. **No-Upfront** does not require payment in advance, but has a higher monthly cost and with lower discount.

More specifically, the pricing policy concerning Amazon's on-demand and reserved T3xlarge instance is presented in Table 1 [15]. T3xlarge can be purchased for 3-year term.

Table 1. Pricing of T3.XLarge instance by Amazon EC (Region(Europe),Linux)

Pricing strategy	Payment option	Upfront $	Monthly $	Period $	Total $	Discount (%) *
3 Year billing						
Compute savings lans	Full upfront	1,646.40	-	-	1,646.40	67.32
Standard reserved instances	Partial upfront	1,007.00	27.96	1,006.56	2,013.56	60.03
EC2 instance savings lans	No upfront	-	60.44	2,175.84	2,175.84	56.81
On-demand instances	-	-	139.94	5,037.84	5,037.84	0.00

*discount on the on-demand price of the billing period.

According to Table 1 users that adopt no upfront payment for purchasing T3.XLarge instance obtain discount ranging 36.99%–56.81% over the on-demand price. In addition, partial upfront requires users to pay almost 50% of the all upfront price plus a monthly cost, and offers a slightly higher discount (60.03%). Finally, Full Upfront option requires users to pay the entire cost of the T3.XLarge instance in advance, enjoying the largest discount (67.32%). For the implementation of the model, broker reserves the T3.XLarge instance by Amazon EC and pays in advance, using Full Upfront option at cost $P_{res} = 1,646.40\$$ for the 3-year term. According to table 1, the chosen payment option is the most advantageous solution for broker, since the broker gains the maximum discount and then can maximize the profit potential.

Amazon offers various instances, however without loss of generality, the T3.XLarge instance was chosen for the implementation of the model with an average price of all Europe regions. It is a low cost burstable general purpose instance type that provides a baseline level of CPU performance with the ability to burst CPU usage at any time for as long as required [17]. Based on the proposed model, broker's profit potential is not essentially affected by the chosen instance.

4.2 Broker Business Model

Broker represents a model that can be extended to many different markets and implementations. The proposed approach introduces a business model that aims to be profitable by investing money in reserving Amazon's VMs and selling them to end users. Broker's economic viability and profitability depend upon the pricing policy; the selling price should be at a level that will eventually cover the cost and produce profit [11].

Amazon offers RIs that can be purchased for 1-year and 3-year terms. Broker can offer RIs that can be purchased for a shorter leasing time, for example 3-month, 6-month or 18-month terms, thus providing more flexible and cheaper services than Amazon.

Based on the mathematical formulation of the problem, broker's selling price is strongly related to the on-demand price of Amazon and is expected to be lower than this. For example broker can set a selling price at a level of 15% lower than the Amazon's on-demand pricing. Hence and based on Eq. 9 different prices of α can form different levels of P_{sell} and different pricing policies.

In order to examine the profit potential of the proposed pricing policies the financial viability of the investment is initially examined by conducting a break-even point analysis that can be a effective tool to lower the risk and point out the most profitable policy. A break-even point corresponds to the quantity that should be offered in order to cover the fixed and variable costs and defines the point that the investment will generate a positive return [24]. It is the point at which total cost and total revenue are equal [18].

The break-even point analysis takes into consideration the fixed cost of the investment and the proposed selling prices, described by Eq. 9 and estimates the break-even point of each pricing policy. The break-even point analysis is conducted for the Amazon EC2 3-year term reserved T3.Xlarge instance as shown in Table 1 and broker choose the Full Up Front payment option.

Since the financial viability of the investment has been evaluated the profit potential is explored. Return of Investment (ROI) is adopted in order to examine the potential return from the current investment for each proposed pricing policy. ROI is a financial metric that is widely used to measure the probability of gaining a return from an investment. It is a ratio between net income (over a period) and investment costs [10].

Broker in order to be flexible and competitive in the cloud marker can modify the pricing strategy when the break-even point is reached. Three (3) pricing policies are proposed that alter broker's initial pricing policy. The proposed policies are based on the purchase intentions of the consumers and sellers in the market [8,30]

- **Greedy Pricing:** The corresponding scenario can be adopted when the demand for cloud resources is high and the availability is low, accompanied by a low market competition. Under those circumstances, the broker can modify the pricing policy with a price similar to the initial provider. The scenario can be used when demand by end-users is high like the surge in usage that COVID-19 has caused [12].

$$P_{sell}(t) = P_{ond}(t) \qquad (10)$$

- **Dynamic Pricing:** The selling price P_{sell} is reduced, following an exponential distribution over time periods. A dynamic strategy aims to locate the optimum price point at any time. It can be adopted in the case of increased availability of resources and also is indicated when the selling price is varied due to technology evolution [8].

$$P_{sell}(t) = P_{ond}(t)/2^x \quad x = 1, 2, 3...t, \text{time periods} \qquad (11)$$

– **Spot-Low Pricing:** The specific pricing policy is inspired by Amazon Spot Instances, without including bidding. Spot instance pricing can be almost 90% cheaper than the on-demand equivalent [16]. Into this context, the broker aims to be competitive by modifying the selling price P_{sell}. The broker minimizes the coefficient α of Eq. 9 and offers VMs in a highly competitive price, without having unused resources. This policy can increase the number of end-users, increase broker's market share [30] and offers minimum guaranteed profit.

$$P_{sell}(t) = \alpha * P_{ond}(t) \text{ , where } \alpha \approx 0 \tag{12}$$

4.3   Evaluation - Results

As mentioned above, the broker reserves instances from Amazon and leases them to users, seeking for a pricing policy that will boost its profitability. In order to be flexible and competitive to Amazon, it offers to users RIs for a shorter leasing time For demonstration reasons and without loss of generality the evaluation of the model is based on a 6-month (semester) leasing. According to the mathematical formulation of the model, the broker's selling price P_{sell} is strongly related to Amazon's on-demand price P_{ond}. According to the evolution of the market, Amazon's EC2 prices have dropped 10.5% annually during the last years [19]. However, in the current case study the annual on-demand price reduction is assumed to be equal to 8% rather than 10.5%. This is because the COVID-19 pandemic has accelerated cloud adoption, so a smaller price reduction could be expected to be adopted, as result of the resources demand increase [12]. Amazon's on-demand price currently equals to 0.1856 $/per hour [14], hence taking into account the rate of price reduction per semester, P_{ond} price per semester was estimated.

Therefore Amazon's on-demand price per semester is estimated and presented in Table 2.

Table 2. Assumptions on price evolution

Duration (Semesters)	Price reduction	Pond/Hour	P_{ond}
1st	0.00%	0.1856 $	801.79 $
2nd	4.00%	0.1782 $	769.72 $
3rd	4.00%	0.1708 $	737.65 $
4th	4.50%	0.1624 $	701.57 $
5th	5.25%	0.1527 $	659.47 $
6th	5.25%	0.1429 $	617.38 $

Broker chooses to lease resources from Amazon, since Amazon is the leader in the cloud market and offers numerous IaaS solutions and various payment options. Table 1 presents its pricing policy for T3.xlarge instance, including all the possible payment options. Based on Table 1 the most advantageous pricing policy of the T3.xlarge was selected to be evaluated within the context of the proposed model. More specifically, the chosen reserved instances is a 3-year term of T3.xlarge at a cost of 1,646.40\$, adopting the Full Upfront payment option. According to Table 1 broker gains a significant discount (67.32%), which corresponds to the broker's surplus. As mentioned in the mathematical formulation section, the broker reserves Q instances, however for simplicity and demonstration reasons the present case study is based on leasing only one T3.xlarge instance.

As far as pricing is concerned, a broker seeks to set the selling prices that will help to achieve profit maximization. Its selling price, P_{sell}, is expected to be lower than Amazon's on-demand pricing and is expressed by the coefficient α of the Eq. 9. Broker can set various values to α and define the corresponding pricing policies. Examining each policy the profit potential and consumer surplus are pointed out. For example if coefficient *alpha* equals to 71.30% then broker's selling price is 28.7% lower than Amazon's on demand price. Figure 3 illustrates the selling price for a specific α and the price evolution of Amazon's on-demand price. The specific pricing policy reaches break-even point at 18 months, therefore the area IC corresponds to the investment cost, the P_{res} price. The area (P) describes broker's profit and finally area CS displays consumer surplus.

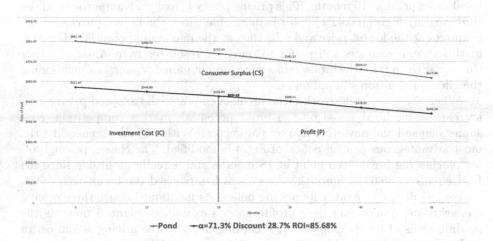

Fig. 3. Profit model for $\alpha = 71.3\%$

Figure 4 illustrates different pricing policies, based on different values of the coefficient *alpha* Since the investment cost is fixed, the values of *alpha* contribute significantly to profit maximization. The investment cost, together with the profit and the consumer surplus can be highlighted for each pricing policy.

According to Fig. 4 the coefficient *alpha* ranges between 38.40% and 100%. The pricing policy which corresponds to the minimum coefficient α (38.40%)

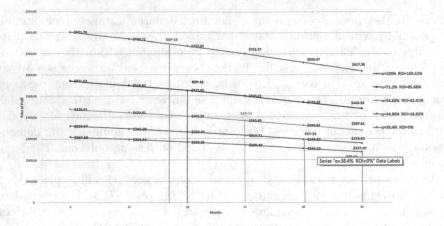

Fig. 4. Profit maximization model

makes the investment viable and reaches the break-even point at the end of the investment evaluation, at the end of the 36 months. Despite the fact that the selling price is 61.6% lower than Amazon and the customer surplus is the highest in this case, the broker has no profit. When the broker's selling price is equal to Amazon's on-demand price, then the *alpha* is 100%. The investment reaches the break-even point at 15 months. This pricing policy is really advantageous and the ROI is really high (160.42%). This is justifiable, since the broker purchased the resources at the lowest price and sells then at the maximum potential. However, in this case, consumers will prefer to purchase resources from Amazon rather than lease them from the broker, since there do not gain discount, not mentioning the effect of Amazon's brand name.

When the investment reaches the break-even point, the adopted pricing policy can be modified based on the profit potential, market competition, consumer demand and any other market parameters. Without loss of generality, the most advantageous pricing policy of Fig. 4 is modified. The chosen pricing policy reaches the break-even point at 18 months and is really profitable since the ROI equals to 85.68%. Since the investment has reached the break-even point, broker can decide to modify its pricing policy. As mentioned above three pricing scenarios are applied and their profitability is examined. Figure 5 presents the modifications of the pricing policy, according to the three pricing scenarios. In addition the profits of each policy are estimated and highlighted.

A significantly high profit is related to the Greedy scenario. In this case Amazon and the broker sell at the same price and the estimated Return of Investment (ROI) is equal to 120%.

In the case of a competitive market, the broker needs to adopt a competition-based pricing strategy, which is mainly characterized by low retail prices. A low selling price can ensure that the investment will be profitable and broker's market share can be increased. In the Dynamic and Spot-Low scenarios, the broker drops the selling prices significantly. In the Dynamic scenario, the selling price

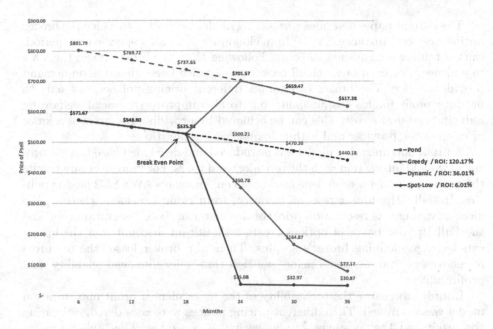

Fig. 5. Alternative pricing scenarios after the break-even point

is reduced following an exponential distribution and the ROI of the Dynamic scenario equals to 36%. Initially, the selling price is 28.7% lower then Amazon's price. Then, there is a price reduction and the selling price for the last 3 semesters is 50%, 75% and 87.5% lower than Amazon's pricing respectively. Finally, in the Spot-Low scenario, the broker offers resources at a price level of 95% lower than Amazon. In this case, its profit is limited, since the ROI equals only to 6%. However, this policy can increase significantly broker's market share and establish a share in the cloud market.

If the broker decides to keep the initial pricing policy, offering the resources at a level of 28.7% lower than Amazon on-demand pricing, profits are higher than by adopting Dynamic and Spot-Low scenarios. However, the Dynamic and Low Pricing scenarios are based on low and more flexible pricing that can increase the broker's market shares.

5   Conclusions

The exponential increasing adoption of IaaS market has significantly contributed to the growth of the cloud broker market. In addition, the unprecedented scenario of COVID19 pandemic has upgraded the role and the contribution of broker to the cloud market. Cloud broker is an IT role and business model and acts as an intermediary between cloud providers and end users [26]. The business model aims to be viable and profitable, based on a proper pricing policy.

The current paper describes a brokering model, according to which the broker initially reserves instances (VMs) from cloud providers for a specific time period, thus obtaining a significant discount. Following that, the broker leases the VMs to end-users, or even other cloud brokers, at a price lower than the on-demand provider's price. The broker can adopts different pricing policies, not only to produce profit for his sustainability but to also improve the social welfare by reducing end-user's cost. This can be achieved by providing resources at a lower price than the provider and with a flexible leasing duration.

A profit maximization model was introduced and developed based on the broker's two-fold interaction with the providers and users. For more accurate results the proposed model was implemented based on Amazon's AWS EC2 pricing policies. Initially, the broker reserves resources from cloud providers, choosing the most advantageous reservation price for 3-year terms. The reservation time and the Full Upfront payment options create a significant discount that the broker can leverage, defining broker's surplus. Then, the broker leases the resources to end-users and defines pricing policies that offer financial viability and profitability.

In order to ensure the profitability of the investment a profit maximization model was examined. Then different pricing polices were considered, estimating the profit and the consumer surplus each one generates. The broker aims to produce profit by leasing the resources at a lower price than the provider's on-demand price, in order to attract end-user not to obtain resources directly by the provider (e.g. Amazon).

Based on the results, with a more adaptable and competitive pricing policy, the broker has the ability to offer significantly lower selling prices than Amazon and generate a considerable profit. It is notable to mention that even with a dramatic price drop returns profits there is a minimum profitability.

As in most cases, there some limitations in this paper. In the above case study the broker receives payments from end-users with a 6-month lease. Also, the assumption that each RI is leased for the whole duration of the study, should be replaced with a mathematical distribution that better expresses demand. Finally, in the future the model can be applied adopting a shorter leasing periods and also calculate profit for RIs that have been obtained for a shorter duration from the provider and a different payment option such as Partial Upfront or No Upfront.

References

1. Alashhab, Z.R., Anbar, M., Singh, M.M., Leau, Y.B., Al-Sai, Z.A., Alhayja'a, S.A.: Impact of coronavirus pandemic crisis on technologies and cloud computing applications. J. Electr. Sci. Technol. **19**,100059 (2020)
2. Amazon: https://aws.amazon.com. Accessed 6 Apr 2021
3. Amazonmarketshare. https://www.statista.com/chart/18819/worldwide-market-share-of-leading-cloud-infrastructure-service-providers/. Accessed 7 Apr 2021
4. Ambati, P., Irwin, D., Shenoy, P.: No reservations: a first look at amazon's reserved instance marketplace. In: 12th USENIX Workshop on Hot Topics in Cloud Computing (HotCloud 2020) (2020)

5. Azure, M.: https://azure.microsoft.com/en-us/. Accessed 6 Apr 2021
6. Boulding, K.E.: The concept of economic surplus. Am. Econ. Rev. **35**(5), 851–869 (1945)
7. Buyya, R., Yeo, C.S., Venugopal, S., Broberg, J., Brandic, I.: Cloud computing and emerging it platforms: vision, hype, and reality for delivering computing as the 5th utility. Fut. Gene. Comput. Syst. **25**(6), 599–616 (2009)
8. Elmaghraby, W., Keskinocak, P.: Dynamic pricing in the presence of inventory considerations: research overview, current practices, and future directions. Manag. Sci. **49**(10), 1287–1309 (2003)
9. Filiopoulou, E., Mitropoulou, P., Michalakelis, C., Nikolaidou, M.: The rise of cloud brokerage: business model, profit making and cost savings. In: Bañares, J.Á., Tserpes, K., Altmann, J. (eds.) GECON 2016. LNCS, vol. 10382, pp. 19–32. Springer, Cham (2017). https://doi.org/10.1007/978-3-319-61920-0_2
10. Friedlob, G.T., Plewa Jr., F.J.: Understanding Return on Investment. John Wiley & Sons, Hoboken (1996)
11. Hanna, N., Dodge, H.R.: Pricing: Policies and Procedures. Macmillan International Higher Education, London (2017)
12. Cloud Services Global Market Report 2021: COVID 19 Impact and Recovery to 2030. https://www.reportlinker.com/p06009776/Cloud-Services-Global-Market-Report-COVID-19-Impact-and-Recovery-to.html. Accessed 28 Apr 2021
13. Reserved Instances. https://docs.aws.amazon.com/AWSEC2/latest/UserGuide/ec2-reserved-instances.html. Accessed 6 Apr 2021
14. On Demand Instances. https://docs.aws.amazon.com/AWSEC2/latest/UserGuide/ec2-on-demand-instances.html. Accessed 6 Apr 2021
15. Reserved Instances. https://aws.amazon.com/ec2/pricing/reserved-instances/pricing/. Accessed 6 Apr 2021
16. Amazon EC2 Spot instances. https://aws.amazon.com/ec2/spot/pricing/
17. Amazon EC2 T3 Instances. https://aws.amazon.com/ec2/instance-types/t3/
18. Kampf, R., Majerčák, P., Švagr, P.: Application of break-even point analysis. NAŠE MORE: znanstveni časopis za more i pomorstvo **63**(3 Special Issue), 126–128 (2016)
19. Llorente, I.M.: The limits to cloud price reduction. IEEE Cloud Comput. **4**(3), 8–13 (2017)
20. marketsandmarket. https://www.marketsandmarkets.com/Market-Reports/covid-19-impact-on-cloud-computing-market-86614844.html
21. Mei, J., Li, K., Tong, Z., Li, Q., Li, K.: Profit maximization for cloud brokers in cloud computing. IEEE Trans. Parallel Distrib. Syst. **30**(1), 190–203 (2018)
22. Nesmachnow, S., Iturriaga, S., Dorronsoro, B.: Efficient heuristics for profit optimization of virtual cloud brokers. IEEE Comput. Intell. Mag. **10**(1), 33–43 (2015)
23. GC Platform. https://azure.microsoft.com/en-us/
24. Reinhardt, U.E.: Break-even analysis for lockheed's Tri Star: an application of financial theory. J. Fin. **28**(4), 821–838 (1973)
25. Research and Markets: Cloud services brokerage market - growth, trends, Covid-19 impact, and forecasts (2021–2026). https://www.researchandmarkets.com/reports4591657/cloud-services-brokerage-market-growth-trends
26. Saha, G., Pasumarthy, R.: Maximizing profit of cloud brokers under quantized billing cycles: a dynamic pricing strategy based on ski-rental problem. In: 2015 53rd Annual Allerton Conference on Communication, Control, and Computing (Allerton), pp. 1000–1007 IEEE (2015)
27. Share, I.M.: https://www.statista.com/statistics/258718/market-growth-forecast-of-public-it-cloud-services-worldwide/

28. Shinde, V., Patil, A., Kodre, S., Bhandari, G., et al.: Participation of cloud broker in cloud computing to achieve maximum profit. Int. J. Res. Anal. Rev. **5**(4), 1109–1112 (2018)
29. Wang, X., et al.: Maximizing the profit of cloud broker with priority aware pricing. In: 2017 IEEE 23rd International Conference on Parallel and Distributed Systems (ICPADS), pp. 511–518. IEEE (2017)
30. White, T.B., Yuan, H.: Building trust to increase purchase intentions: the signaling impact of low pricing policies. J. Consumer Psychol. **22**(3), 384–394 (2012)
31. Zhang, R., Wu, K., Li, M., Wang, J.: Online resource scheduling under concave pricing for cloud computing. IEEE Trans. Paralle.l Distrib. Syst. **27**(4), 1131–1145 (2015)

An Experimental Analysis of Function Performance with Resource Allocation on Serverless Platform

Yonghe Zhang[1,2], Kejiang Ye[1(✉)], and Cheng-Zhong Xu[3]

[1] Guangdong-Hong Kong-Macao Joint Laboratory of Human-Machine Intelligence-Synergy Systems, Shenzhen Institute of Advanced Technology, Chinese Academy of Sciences, Shenzhen 518055, China
{yh.zhang,kj.ye}@siat.ac.cn
[2] University of Chinese Academy of Sciences, Beijing 100049, China
[3] State Key Laboratory of IoT for Smart City, University of Macau, Macau SAR, China
czxu@um.edu.mo

Abstract. Serverless computing is currently receiving much attention from both academia and industry. It has a straightforward interface that abstracts the complex internal structure of cloud computing resource usage and configuration. The fine grained pay-per-use model of serverless computing can dramatically reduce the cost of using cloud computing resources for users. Thus, today more and more traditional cloud applications are moving to the serverless architecture. In serverless computing, *functions* executing in containers are the basic unit of scheduling. However, the impact of resource allocation on function performance in serverless platform is still not clear. It is very challenging to improve the function performance while reducing the resource costs in serverless platform. In this paper, we select several typical workloads in serverless and analyze the function performance by controlling the CPU and memory resources. Experimental results reveal the impact of resource allocation on the performance of different types of functions. We also classify the functions in serverless according to their dependence on CPU resources and memory resources.

Keywords: Cloud native · Serverless computing · Container · Performance analysis

1 Introduction

Serverless computing is emerging as a new trend for cloud computing, which frees developers from managing servers and has been favored by many cloud service providers, including Amazon [1], IBM [2], Microsoft [3], and Google [4]. In serverless computing, *functions* serve as the most basic unit of computation. A complete application is made up of a series of functions, each of which is called

© Springer Nature Switzerland AG 2022
K. Ye and L.-J. Zhang (Eds.): CLOUD 2021, LNCS 12989, pp. 17–31, 2022.
https://doi.org/10.1007/978-3-030-96326-2_2

one or more times. When a service request is received, the serverless platform allocates a temporary sandbox in which user-defined functions are instantiated to process the request, and then returns the result to the user. Serverless computing allows developers to focus entirely on their application logic without having to manage a variety of cumbersome cloud computing resources. In addition, cloud providers can manage their resources more efficiently using serverless computing. The use of a serverless computing architecture is a giant leap forward for both cloud service providers and service users. Serverless computing enables developers to develop more efficient and cloud service providers to control resources at a finer granularity, scale up and down more quickly, and improve resource utilization. The benefits of serverless computing have led the traditional software architectures to shift to serverless computing architectures.

The rational allocation of resources in various forms of cloud computing services has been a hot issue that has been studied in academia or industry. For users, a more rational resource allocation means lower-cost cloud computing services. For cloud providers, a better resource allocation strategy allows them to have the higher computing power for the same server configuration, which also means higher profits. In traditional cloud computing, the virtual machine is the basic unit of service provided by the cloud service provider. However, in serverless computing, the container becomes the basic unit for executing functions. In this new computing paradigm, the impact of resource allocation on the performance of function execution is still not clear. In this paper, we use various types of functions as workloads to test the function execution time under different resource configurations and analyze the impact of computer resources on function performance. We also classify the functions according to their dependence on CPU resources and memory resources.

The rest of this paper is organized as follows: Sect. 2 introduces the background and related work; Sect. 3 describes the design of experiment; Sect. 4 presents the experiment results and discussion; Finally, we conclude the paper in Sect. 5.

2   Background and Related Work

2.1   Container

In serverless framework, container technology is used instead of traditional virtual machines as the most basic execution and scheduling unit. In traditional virtualization, the hypervisor virtualizes the physical hardware. The result is that each virtual machine contains a guest operating system, a virtual copy of the hardware required for the operating system to run, and an application with its associated libraries and dependencies. Virtual machines with different operating systems can run on the same physical server. Rather than virtualizing the underlying hardware, containers [5] virtualize the operating system, so each individual container contains only the application and its libraries and dependencies. Containers are small, fast and portable because, unlike virtual machines, they do not need to include the guest operating system in each instance, but can instead

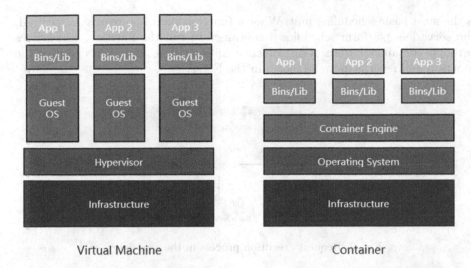

Fig. 1. Virtual machines vs containers

leverage the functionality and resources of the host operating system. Container technology has some relative loss of isolation, but containers are lighter than virtual machines. Using container technology as the infrastructure for the cloud platform can lead to powerful scale-up and scale-down capabilities and rapid response times. The comparison of containers and virtual machines is shown in the Fig. 1.

The two most essential technologies in containers are cgroups [6], a kernel function that controls and limits the use of resources for one or more process groups, and systemd, which is used to initialize the system to set up user controls and manage their processes. Compared to traditional virtual machines, containers are lighter, faster to start, simpler to deploy, and more migratable. The container technology represented by Docker container has greatly accelerated the development of cloud computing. In recent years, with the advent of serverless technology, there are even some dedicated containers for serverless, such as Firecracker [7].

2.2 Serverless

Cloud computing [8] infrastructure has evolved from monolithic, clustered, and distributed architectures to distributed microservice architectures. As the architecture evolved, applications were continuously split up, and an extensive application gradually became a combination of several smaller applications. Finer granularity of segmentation means that the cloud platform can scale up and down for some parts of the application individually. It results in a cloud platform with higher resource utilization and a more rational way of resource allocation. It brings lower costs to users and higher profits to cloud computing service providers. In this background, serverless was born, and in serverless, a function is the most basic scheduling unit. When a function execution request is received, the serverless platform schedules a container to run the function, which goes through container initialization, runtime initialization, and then executes the function and returns data, as shown in the Fig. 2.

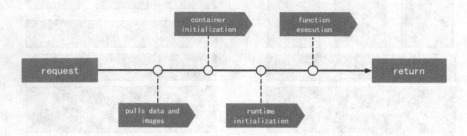

Fig. 2. Request execution process in the container

As academia and industry continue to focus on serverless, a variety of serverless frameworks continue to emerge. Such as, apache provides the open-source serverless framework openwhisk, CNCF [9] provides the open-source framework openfaas [10], knative [11] and so on. In our experiments, we chose the openwhisk framework as the experimental platform because it is a representative serverless framework that has undergone large-scale commercial adoption. Apache OpenWhisk is an open source, distributed Serverless platform that executes functions in response to events at any scale. OpenWhisk manages the infrastructure, servers and scaling using Docker containers. The architecture of Openwhisk is shown in the Fig. 3.

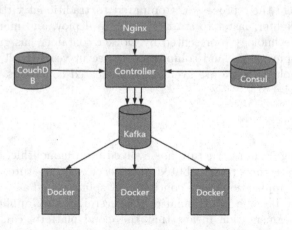

Fig. 3. The architecture of Openwhisk

2.3   Related Work

Ye et al. [12,13] investigated the effect of system parameters on the application's performance in the container using machine learning algorithms and model the performance of the application running in the container. This is a valuable study, but in a serverless environment, applications running in containers will behave differently. Felter et al. [14] explored the performance of traditional virtual machine (VM) deployments and compared it to the use of Linux containers. The results show that in almost all cases, containers perform as well or better than VMs. We investigated the performance of containers in the serverless environment at the application level. Ye et al. [13] proposes a performance prediction model based on the Support Vector Regression (SVR) to predict the application performance with different configurations and resource competition settings. Padala et al. [15] proposes a moving average model that can be automatically regressed and used to represent the relationship between an application's performance and its resource allocation. The accuracy of these models is still a little lacking. Lin et al. [16] proposes a new construct to formally define a serverless application workflow, and then implement analytical models to predict the average end-to-end response time and the cost of the workflow. There are a variety of applications in serverless environments, and this model is not applicable in all cases. Akhtaret et al. [17] proposes a framework, COSE, which uses Bayesian optimization techniques to find the best configuration for serverless functions. COSE uses statistical learning techniques to intelligently collect samples and predict serverless functions' cost and execution time. Zhang et al. [18] presents an engine for recommending configurations for Hadoop on container-driven clouds. It has a better performance in big data applications but is not applicable to all applications.

In order to optimize the efficiency of the load running in the container, there are many related studies. Adam et al. [19] proposed a stochastic resource provisioning for containerized multi-tier web services in clouds. Higgins et al. [20] evaluates the performance of Docker containers as runtimes for high-performance parallel execution. Arnautov et al. [21] described SCONE, a secure container mechanism for Docker that uses the SGX trusted execution support of Intel CPUs to protect container processes from outside attacks. Harter et al. [22] proposed Slacker, a new Docker storage driver optimized for fast container startup. Docker workers quickly provision container storage using backend clones and minimize startup latency by lazily fetching container data.

3   Experiment Design

In this section, we describe the experimental design in detail. For the experimental environment, we built kubernetes on an Ubuntu system and run the serverless framework on kubernetes. We choose Openwhisk as our experimental platform. Openwhisk, an open-source serverless framework, has the advantages of easy deployment, ease of use, and robust scalability. The general architecture of our experiments is shown in Fig. 4.

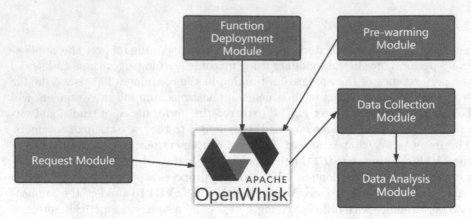

Fig. 4. Experimental system architecture

Our experimental system is divided into five main modules. They are as follows:

- **Function Deployment Module.** The function deployment module is responsible for submitting the functions needed for the experiment to openwhisk. Openwhisk receives the request and stores the function-related information in the database for invocation.
- **Request Module.** The request module is responsible for sending requests to openwhisk to executive functions. When the request is passed to openwhisk via kubernetes, openwhisk parses the request information, searches the corresponding function from the database, and schedules the function to the container for execution.
- **Data Collection Module.** The data collection module will collect metrics data about the function during execution and then save the data to the database.
- **Data Analysis Module.** The data analysis module takes out the corresponding data from the database, cleans the useless data, and analyzes it.
- **Pre-warming Module.** The pre-warming module is responsible for pre-warming the container before the start of the experiment. Using a warmed-up container for experiments can avoid large deviations in the experimental results caused by a cold start of the container.

4   Experimental Results and Discussion

In this section, we choose some typical functions in serverless architecture as the load for our evaluation of serverless performance. In Sect. 4.1, we use a CPU-intensive function, where the size of memory does not affect the runtime of the function when it is invoked, but the CPU resources directly affect the efficiency of the function. In Sect. 4.2, we use a memory-intensive function. This means that

Table 1. The functions used in our experiment

Category	Description	Language
CPU-intensive function	Compute complex mathematical formulas using multiple threads	Python
Memory-intensive function	Summation of large integer arrays	Java
Image processing application	Image recognition	Java
Big data processing function	Word frequency statistics	Python

the execution time of the function is heavily influenced by memory. In Sect. 4.3, we choose a serverless application for image processing, which is common in the real world. The application consists of a chain of five individual functions that perform all the parts of image processing. In Sect. 4.4, we have chosen a typical function in a big data application, whose performance is affected by both CPU and memory resources. All the functions in our experiment is shown in Table 1. To eliminate unpredictable delays caused by the container cold start process, we run several simulations with the same load before each experiment to allow the container to warm up for a period of time in advance to avoid unnecessary delays. In this paper, we use a server with a 10-core, 20-thread Intel Core i9-10900K CPU which has 20 MB of L3 cache. The server has 64 GB of 2133 MHz DDR4 RAM connected to four channels, which has been sufficient for our experiments both regarding memory capacity and available CPU resource.

4.1 CPU-Intensive Function

In this part, we use a python function as the serverless workload that implements mathematical calculations in a multi-threaded context. The serverless container is warmed up before the experiment to eliminate unpredictable delays during the cold start, and after the container starts, we control the CPU resources by controlling the LimitRange of k8s under the namespace of OpenWhisk. In this experiment, the initial CPU resource we assign to the container is 1000 m, which means that the container can get the resources of one thousand millicores or one CPU core, and then we increase the CPU resource limit set in the LimitRange in turn to determine the performance of the function workload.

Figure 5 shows the function workloads' performance when the resource limit of CPU is adjusted from 1000 m to 10000 m. The horizontal coordinate of Fig. 5 represents the CPU resources available to the serverless container, and the vertical coordinate represents the runtime of the workload in the corresponding configuration. We perform one hundred experiments for each CPU configuration and round off the maximum and minimum values to ensure the measurement data's accuracy. The experiments show that when the allocated CPU resources are inadequate, each time the CPU limit in LimitRange increases, the function's runtime will significantly reduce. However, when the container can use more CPU resources, the function's runtime will converge to a stable value, and there

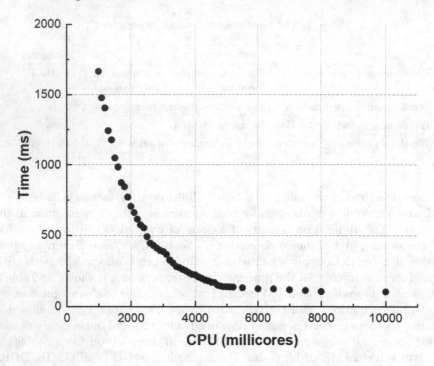

Fig. 5. Performance of CPU-intensive functions

will be no significant performance improvement even if the CPU resources are increased.

4.2 Memory-Intensive Function

In this part, we use a function written in Java as the workload. This function generates a large integer array during running and thus has a high dependency on memory resources. We use the -m parameter of *wsk* to adjust the size of the function memory. We set the minimum memory value to 220 MB and the maximum memory value to 480 MB, and within this range we set the function's available memory value at fixed intervals. Function performance is shown in Fig. 6. The horizontal coordinate in Fig. 6 represents the maximum memory size that the function can use for execution, and the vertical coordinate represents the function execution time with the corresponding memory configuration. For each result we performed multiple experiments to take the average.

The experimental results show that when the memory resources allocated by a function are small, gradually increasing the allocation of memory resources can significantly improve the execution performance of the function, which is somewhat similar to the results of CPU-intensive. However, the performance of the function fluctuates considerably on the same level when memory resources are allocated to a certain value. At this point, the memory resources of the

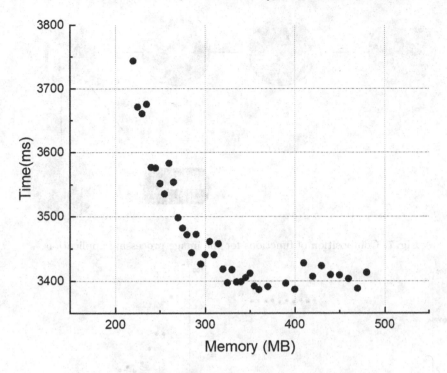

Fig. 6. Performance of memory-intensive functions

function have been fully satisfied, and continuing to increase memory resources does not improve the efficiency of the function's execution.

4.3 AI Application Function

Image processing is one of the more widely used serverless AI applications. In this part, we have chosen a typical image processing program consisting of a complete chain of function calls from five functions. When OpenWhisk receives a request to execute this image processing application, the first function is triggered, which extracts the metadata from the image and passes the result to the following function to verify the image format. The following function detects the objects in the image, and the last two functions are responsible for storing and returning the result. The function composition of the entire application is shown in Fig. 7.

We have done two sets of experiments on this image processing application for CPU resources and memory resources respectively. One set of experiments fixes the maximum memory resource that the function can use and varies the CPU resource, and the other set of experiments fixes the CPU resource and varies the maximum memory that the function can use. The experimental results are shown in Fig. 8.

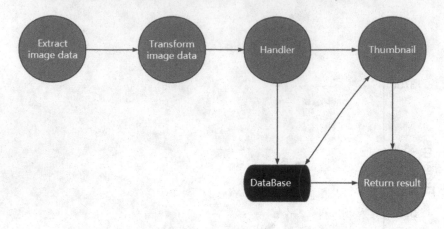

Fig. 7. Composition of functions for the image processing application

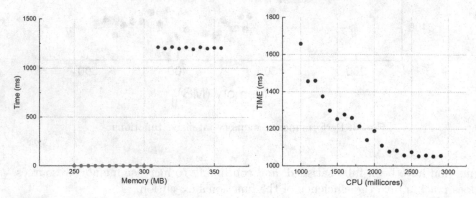

Fig. 8. Experimental results of the image processing application (Color figure online)

The experimental results show that the effect of CPU resources on the function execution performance of this image processing program is similar to the previous experiments in Sect. 4.1. In contrast, the effect of memory resources on the function performance is very different from the previous experiments in Sect. 4.2. The red dots in the left panel of Fig. 8 represent applications that do not run properly in this configuration. The image processing application returns the correct value when the available allocated memory resources of the function are around 310 MB. When the function allocates more than 310 MB of memory, the execution time of the function continues to fluctuate at 1200 ms, and increasing the available memory for the function does not improve the efficiency of the function execution.

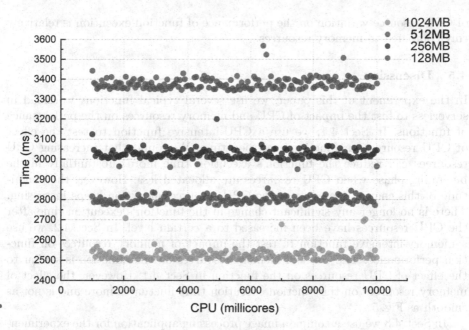

Fig. 9. Comparative experimental results of image processing applications (Color figure online)

4.4   Big Data Processing Function

In recent years, with the increasing popularity of the Internet, big data has been developing hot. With the dramatic increase in Internet data, the clusters of big data processing applications are becoming increasingly complex. In order to overcome the shortcomings of the traditional approach, big data applications have also started to use serverless architecture gradually. Therefore, in this section, we choose a typical function from a big data application as the workload for this experiment, which implements counting the frequency of each word occurring in the cluttered data. In this experiment, we conducted a total of four sets of experiments by allocating different memory resources, and the results are shown in the Fig. 9. The horizontal coordinate represents the CPU resources available to the serverless container, and the vertical coordinate represents the runtime of the workload under the corresponding configuration. And the four different colored dots represent the different memory resource allocation. The red dot is set to 128 MB of available memory resources, the blue dot is set to 256 MB, the green dot is set to 512 MB, and the orange dot is set to 1024 MB.

The experimental results show that the execution time of this function has a large difference under different memory settings. However, with the same memory settings, the function's runtime is always at the same level, with no significant fluctuations except for occasional outliers. It can be seen that the impact of CPU resource variation on the performance of function execution is relatively tiny compared to memory resources.

4.5 Discussion

In the experiment of this paper, we use several typical functions workload in serverless to test the impact of CPU and memory resources on the performance of functions. In Sect. 4.1, we use a CPU-intensive function to test the effect of CPU resources on function execution time. We found that increasing CPU resources can reduce the function's execution time more substantially in the beginning phase when CPU resources are allocated less. However, the magnitude of this change decreases as the CPU resource allocation keeps increasing. There is no longer any significant change in the function's execution time after the CPU resources have been increased to a certain level. In Sect. 4.2, we use a memory-intensive function to test the impact of memory resources on function performance. The effect of memory resources on this function is similar to the effect of CPU resources on the function in Sect. 4.1. However, the effect of memory resources on the function execution time fluctuates more and is not as smooth as Fig. 5.

In Sect. 4.3 we use a common image processing application for the experimental workload, consisting of several functions. The CPU impact on this application is the same as the results in Sect. 4.1. The results of this experiment differ significantly from the results of the memory-intensive experiment in Sect. 4.2. In the left figure of Fig. 8, when the memory resource allocation is less than 310 MB, the image processing program does not run properly. And when the function allocates memory resources greater than 310 MB, the function's running time will be fixed at about 1200 ms. Continuously increasing the memory resources allocated by a function does not improve the efficiency of the function's performance. This phenomenon is because the container does not have enough memory space to load the image into memory when the function allocates less than 310 MB of memory resources. Moreover, once the container loads the image into memory, adding more memory resources does not help the function perform effectively; this is why the cliff-like experimental image in the left panel of Fig. 8 appears.

In the experiments with big data functions in Sect. 4.4, we did four sets of experiments depending on the memory allocation of the functions. In each set of experiments, the continuous increase in CPU resources did not improve the efficiency of function execution, and the function execution time was maintained within a specific range without significant fluctuations. However, the function execution time varies widely between each set of experiments. This phenomenon is because this big data processing function has a high dependence on memory resources, while the CPU resources have little impact on the execution time of this function.

By summarizing the experimental results of this paper, we can classify the functions into low CPU resource-dependent type and high CPU resource-dependent type according to the CPU resource dependency of functions. We can also classify the functions into fixed memory requirement type and non-fixed memory requirement type according to their dependence on memory resources. Classifying the functions running in a serverless environment in terms of the relationship between the resources they require and their performance is an extremely important reference for resource allocation policy optimization, load performance prediction, and other areas. The classification is shown in the Table 2.

Table 2. Function classification

Resource type	Category	Description
CPU	Low CPU resource-dependent type	CPU resources have less impact on function performance
	High CPU resource-dependent type	CPU resources have a phased effect on function performance
Memory	Fixed memory requirement type	Memory resources no longer have an impact on function performance after reaching a fixed value
	Non-fixed memory requirement type	Memory resources have a phased effect on function performance

5   Conclusion and Future Work

As serverless continues to grow in popularity, more and more applications use the serverless paradigm to replace traditional development methods. Serverless provides users with a convenient and straightforward interface that eliminates the need for complex operations such as the configuration of the server environment and the management of resources. When the user uses serverless services, they submit a function and select the CPU and memory configuration to use it. However, users have no basis for allocating resources at all, which is likely to waste resources by allocating too many resources and increasing unnecessary costs. It is also possible to have too few resources configured, resulting in lower-than-expected performance or even failure due to under-configuration.

In this paper, we used CPU-intensive function, memory-intensive function, AI application (image processing) function and Big Data processing function as the workload of the experiment to test the performance of the function under different resource configurations. We analyzed the experimental results describing the impact of CPU and memory resources on different types of functions. We then categorized the functions according to their dependency on CPU and memory resources. We classify the functions into low CPU resource-dependent type and high CPU resource-dependent type according to the CPU resource dependency. We can also classify the functions into fixed memory requirement type and non-fixed memory requirement type according to their dependence on memory resources. Our experimental results provide the basis for user configuration of serverless functions to balance performance and cost.

In the future, we will study the main factors that cause different functions to have different sizes of demand on computer resources at the code level to provide a more precise basis for the rational allocation of resources.

Acknowledgment. This work is supported by Key-Area Research and Development Program of Guangdong Province (NO. 2020B010164003), National Natural Science Foundation of China (No. 62072451), Shenzhen Basic Research Program (No. JCYJ2020 0109115418592), Science and Technology Development Fund of Macao S.A.R (FDCT) under number 0015/2019/AKP, and Youth Innovation Promotion Association CAS (NO. 2019349).

References

1. AWS Lambda - Serverless Compute. https://aws.amazon.com/lambda/
2. Apache OpenWhisk (2021). http://openwhisk.apache.org/
3. Azure Functions Serverless Architecture. https://azure.microsoft.com/en-us/services/functions/
4. Google Cloud Function. https://cloud.google.com/functions/
5. Steenken, D., Voß, S., Stahlbock, R.: Container terminal operation and operations research-a classification and literature review. OR Spectr. **26**(1), 3–49 (2004). https://doi.org/10.1007/s00291-003-0157-z
6. cgroups (2021). http://man7.org/linux/man-pages/man7/cgroups.7.html
7. Agache, A., et al.: Firecracker: lightweight virtualization for serverless applications. In: 17th USENIX Symposium on Networked Systems Design and Implementation (NSDI 2020) (2020)
8. Fox, A., et al.: Above the clouds: a Berkeley view of cloud computing. Department of Electrical Engineering and Computer Sciences, University of California, Berkeley, Report no: UCB/EECS-2009-28 (2009)
9. cncf. https://landscape.cncf.io/
10. openfaas. https://www.openfaas.com/
11. knative. https://github.com/knative/docs/
12. Ye, K., Kou, Y., Lu, C., Wang, Y., Xu, C.Z.: Modeling application performance in docker containers using machine learning techniques. In: 2018 IEEE 24th International Conference on Parallel and Distributed Systems (ICPADS), pp. 1–6. IEEE, December 2018
13. Ye, K., Ji, Y.: Performance tuning and modeling for big data applications in docker containers. In: 2017 International Conference on Networking, Architecture, and Storage (NAS). IEEE (2017)
14. Felter, W., et al.: An updated performance comparison of virtual machines and Linux containers. In: 2015 IEEE International Symposium on Performance Analysis of Systems and Software (ISPASS). IEEE (2015)
15. Padala, P., et al.: Adaptive control of virtualized resources in utility computing environments. In: Proceedings of the 2nd ACM SIGOPS/EuroSys European Conference on Computer Systems 2007, pp. 289–302 (2007)
16. Lin, C., Khazaei, H.: Modeling and optimization of performance and cost of serverless applications. IEEE Trans. Parallel Distrib. Syst. **32**(3), 615–632 (2020)
17. Akhtar, N., Raza, A., Ishakian, V., Matta, I.: COSE: configuring serverless functions using statistical learning. In: IEEE INFOCOM 2020-IEEE Conference on Computer Communications, pp. 129–138. IEEE (2020)

18. Zhang, R., Li, M., Hildebrand, D.: Finding the big data sweet spot: towards automatically recommending configurations for hadoop clusters on docker containers. In: 2015 IEEE International Conference on Cloud Engineering. IEEE (2015)
19. Adam, O., Lee, Y.C., Zomaya, A.Y.: Stochastic resource provisioning for containerized multi-tier web services in clouds. IEEE Trans. Parallel Distrib. Syst. **28**(7), 2060–2073 (2016)
20. Higgins, J., Holmes, V., Venters, C.: Orchestrating docker containers in the HPC environment. In: Kunkel, J.M., Ludwig, T. (eds.) ISC High Performance 2015. LNCS, vol. 9137, pp. 506–513. Springer, Cham (2015). https://doi.org/10.1007/978-3-319-20119-1_36
21. Arnautov, S., et al.: SCONE: secure Linux containers with Intel SGX. In: 12th USENIX Symposium on Operating Systems Design and Implementation (OSDI 2016), pp. 689–703 (2016)
22. Harter, T., Salmon, B., Liu, R., Arpaci-Dusseau, A.C., Arpaci-Dusseau, R.H.: Slacker: fast distribution with lazy docker containers. In: 14th USENIX Conference on File and Storage Technologies (FAST 2016), pp. 181–195 (2016)

Electronic Card Localization Algorithm Based on Visible Light Screen Communication

Kao Wen[1,2], Junjian Huang[1], Chan Zhou[1], and Kejiang Ye[1(✉)]

[1] Guangdong-Hong Kong-Macao Joint Laboratory of Human-Machine Intelligence-Synergy Systems, Shenzhen Institute of Advanced Technology, Chinese Academy of Sciences, Shenzhen 518055, China
{kao.wen,jj.huang,chan.zhou,kj.ye}@siat.ac.cn
[2] University of Chinese Academy of Sciences, Beijing 100049, China

Abstract. In recent years, with the continuous advancement of image processing technology and the popularization of camera-equipped devices, methods of using camera positioning have been gradually developed. The camera positioning can avoid the interference of various wireless signals in the indoor environment, and the positioning stability is strong. At the same time, since most indoor environments and mobile terminals have their own cameras, the use of camera positioning also has the advantage of low hardware costs. In this paper, we propose a QR-Code based localization system which employs QR-code to transmit necessary information for localization. In addition, this paper uses a QR-Code to assist positioning, which improves the accuracy of positioning, and uses a rewritten music algorithm to estimate angle. Finally, a positioning scheme with both precision and low-cost is developed.

Keywords: QR-Code · Visible light screen communication · Localization

1 Introduction

At present, self-driving technology has draw much attentions in related industry research. One of the difficulties of self-driving technology is that it is difficult to accurately estimate the distance between vehicles and the mutual location between vehicles during driving and parking. In the current vehicle location research, camera positioning and high-precision radar positioning are widely used. However, the positioning accuracy of the camera is not high and it can not be worked at a long distance. In the mean time, although the positioning effect of high-precision radar is accurate, it is expensive and cannot be applied in the market.

This paper proposes a high-precision, low-cost positioning system based on two-dimensional codes. The first contribution of this paper is to use screen optical communication to assist positioning, which improves the accuracy of positioning. The second contribution point is the use of MUSIC algorithm to estimate the shooting angle, which reduces the error of angle calculation.

© Springer Nature Switzerland AG 2022
K. Ye and L.-J. Zhang (Eds.): CLOUD 2021, LNCS 12989, pp. 32–44, 2022.
https://doi.org/10.1007/978-3-030-96326-2_3

The rest of the paper is organized as follows: Sect. 2 provides a brief summary of related works. Section 3 describes the architecture of the system proposed followed by details of the positioning method which consists of image processing, distance measurement and angle measurement. Section 4 shows the positioning experiments and the discussion of the experimental results. Conclusions are presented in Sect. 5.

2   Related Work

Localization technology is one of the most important and challenging problems in the field of self-driving, and hence a great deal of works is already available in this area. This section mainly looks at related-work in vision based localization techniques. The first task of a vision-based localization technology is to choose a target which can be a natural object or a artificial landmarks. To further narrow down the scope of the literature review, this section concentrates mainly in indoor localization technology that utilize artificial landmarks.

Landmarks are essential for vision-based localization technology, almost all vision-based localization technology requires a target to assist localization. The natural landmark-based approach suffers limitations because it is sensitive to dynamic environmental conditions and requires high computational power for image processing, thus in general extracting features using natural landmarks are considered to be difficult tasks [1]. Alternative solution proposed in the literature is utilizing artificial landmarks, such as unique artificial object or unique pattern for vision-based localization technology. Comparing with natural landmarks, artificial landmarks are easier to be detected and recognized, this can effectively improve the accuracy and precision of recognition.

[2] is similar to our approach in the way it calculates real coordinates for an indoor mobile robot by combining simple artificial landmarks based image information and distance information calculated from Cricket system [3]. To estimate distance, Cricket system uses the time difference of arrival between radio frequency signals and ultrasonic pulses. Comparing with Cricket system, this paper uses QR-Codes only to localize object without using additional infrastructure.

The technique that is being proposed in this paper is low-cost, robust, and high precision. Through experiments, this paper improves the accuracy of the algorithm to the centimeter level.

3   Proposed Positioning System

3.1   System Architecture

The proposed system consist of two parts: Electronic display and Image collector with single camera. The display is a 55 in. screen with two QR-Codes on it. Two QR-Codes are arranged on the left and right of the electronic screen, and the two QR-Codes are symmetrical about the center of the screen. The QR-Code on the left is placed normally, and the QR-Code on the right rotates 90° clockwise to place. The information format of the QR-Code is $\langle x1, x2\rangle$ Supplementary information, where includes the actual size of the QR-Code, the space between the QR-Codes, the relative position between the screen center and the QR-Code, the road conditions and other auxiliary information. Figure 1 gives an example.

The image collector consists of an image acquisition module with a camera and a triangle bracket. The camera module has a software function to deal with camera distortion [4]. The measuring range is 0–5 m, and taking pictures of electronic screen from different angles. See Fig. 2 for details.

Finder pattern

Fig. 1. QR-Code layout, the area in the three black block on the top left, bottom left and top right of the QR-Code are the finder patterns

Fig. 2. Image collector

3.2   Proposed Positioning Method

Image Pre-processing. The image collected by the image collector is a JPG image with 4032×3024 pixels, which contains two QR-Codes on the smart electronic screen. In order to obtain the information needed for calculation from the QR-Code, system first need to preprocess the obtained image to find the exact location of the QR-Code, and then cut out the image at that location and submit it to the QR-Code parser for analysis.

There are two main steps in image pre-processing: image binaryzation and noise filtering.

Image binaryzation: first of all, the image will be binaried by the system, that is, the color RGB image is converted to black-and-white image, and the conversion threshold is calculated by OSTU algorithm [5].

Noise filtering: after getting the binary image, we need to find the region of the QR-Code in the image. Because of the color's difference between the preset background color and the QR-Code is large, the boundary between the images is relatively obvious. So using the image processing method of boundary suppression can separate the QR-Code from the image background easily.

Image boundary suppression specific method is that system first traverse all the boundary points of the image. If the pixel value of these points is 1, it is considered that there is background noise in these places, and the algorithm will change the pixel value of these places to 0 to eliminate these noises. Every time the pixel value of a point is changed to 0, the algorithm will find out whether there is a point with a pixel value of 1 in the surrounding 8 points adjacent to that point. If there is a point, its pixel value will be changed to 0. Since the pixel value of the QR-Code is 1 and the pixel value of the white background around the QR-Code is 0 after image binarization (Fig. 3) (After anti color, black QR-Code pixel value is 1 while white background pixel value is 0), the pixel values of points at the boundary of QR code are all 0. Therefore, after the image boundary suppression processing, the image background will be cleared and the QR code area will be preserved. Figure 4 shows the effect of boundary suppression.

Fig. 3. Image after binaryzation   **Fig. 4.** Image after boundary suppression

In addition, morphologically open image and morphologically close image which are the general method in image processing are be used to filtering noise [6, 7].

Find QR-Code Location. There are two main steps in this section: feature filtering and shape verification.

Feature filtering: to find the location of the QR-Code, the first things is to find the location of finder pattern [8]. As shown in Fig. 2, the QR-Code has three finder patterns [9], each of which contains a black border and a black square. After image pre-processing complete, a lot of independent white pixel areas (the pixel value of the point is 1) are left in the image. The algorithm reserve the area with holes and eliminate the areas without holes. Finally, the area with holes as shown in Fig. 5 is left, which contains three QR-Code finder patterns.

Shape verification: to determine whether the area with holes are finder pattern, the algorithm will verify the shape of these areas. As shown in Fig. 6, from top to bottom, the ratio of the width of the white area to the width of the black area is 1:1:3:1:1. White area corresponds to wave crest and black areas correspond to wave trough, the algorithm detects the width ratio of wave crest to wave trough of all regions with holes to determine whether the region is finder pattern.

Assuming that the ratio between the wave crest and wave trough calculated is x1: x2: x3: x4: x5, the approximation value y calculated by Euclidean distance is:

$$y = \sqrt{(x_1 - 1)^2 + (x_2 - 1)^2 + (x_3 - 3)^2 + (x_4 - 1)^2 + (x_5 - 1)^2} \qquad (1)$$

The simulation results show that when the value of y is less than 0.8, the system can detect the location region of QR-Code accurately. Therefore, the y value is less than 0.8, which is the criterion to determine the finder pattern of the QR-Code.

Because of knowing the arrangement of the QR-Code in advance, it is known that the three finder patterns with smaller abscissa are the three finder patterns of the left QR-Code, and the three finder patterns with larger abscissa are the finder patterns of the right QR-Code. Figure 7 shows the detailed image processing steps.

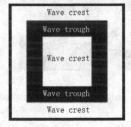

Fig. 5. Reserve the area with hole

Fig. 6. White color block corresponding to wave crest and black color block corresponding to wave trough in finder pattern

Position Correcting. After finding all finder patterns, we can't completely capture the QR-Code image. This is because the QR-Code image on the actual image is mostly parallelogram, the specific location of the QR-Code can not be calculated only by the coordinates of three finder patterns. Therefore, it is necessary to further modify the coordinates of the QR-Code.

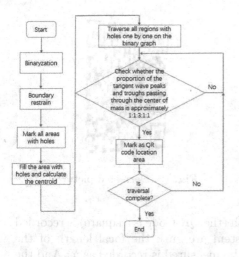

Fig. 7. Image processing flowchart   **Fig. 8.** Coordinate correcting

Figure 8 shows the principle of position correction. Take a single QR-Code as an example. When the center coordinates of the finder patterns of the QR-Code are obtained, the center coordinates of the three finder patterns are recorded as I(a1, b1), J(a2, b2), K(a3, b3) from left to right and from top to bottom. The calculation formula of side length (PX and PY) is as follows equation:

$$PX = 1.27 \times \sqrt{(a_1 - a_2)^2 + (b_1 - b_2)^2} \tag{2}$$

$$PY = 1.27 \times \sqrt{(a_1 - a_3)^2 + (b_1 - b_3)^2} \tag{3}$$

The slope of PX and the PY can be calculated as follow equation:

$$K_X = \frac{b_1 - b_2}{a_1 - a_2} \tag{4}$$

$$K_Y = \frac{b_1 - b_3}{a_1 - a_3} \tag{5}$$

Through the slope and length, the system can accurately locate the specific location of the QR-Code. Figure 9 and Fig. 10 shows the effect before and after position correction. After obtaining the location coordinates of the QR-Code, the left and right QR-Code are intercepted from the binary image, and then transferred to the QR-Code parser for analysis.

Distance Measurement. This paper used Computer Vision based distance measurement system to measurement distance [10]. After the two QR-Code is

Fig. 9. Uncorrected pictures   **Fig. 10.** Corrected pictures

analysised, the actual QR-Code side length (the QR-Code is a square) is recorded as X_1 (all the distance units of the system are cm); the focal length of the camera is recorded as F; The distance to be measured is recorded as Y; And the distance measured from the photos is recorded as X_2. The principle of distance measurement is shown in the Fig. 11:

BC is the actual side length of QR-Code on the electronic screen, and DE is the side length measured on the picture. A pair of similar triangles is formed by ΔABC and ΔADE. The actual measured distance Y is proportional to the focal length F of the camera as follows:

Fig. 11. Principle of camera ranging

$$\frac{Y}{F} = \frac{BC}{DE} \tag{6}$$

The Eq. 6 has the following relations after Transformation:

$$Y = F\frac{BC}{DE} \tag{7}$$

Since the measurement unit of DE in the picture is pixel, to convert the pixel into centimeter, it is necessary to obtain the shooting pixel density of the camera in advance. The pixel density PPI, pixel length cm and pixel PX of the camera are transformed as follows:

$$PPI = \frac{PX}{CM} \tag{8}$$

In this way, the system can get the actual length of the side length through QR-Code analysis, obtain the focal length and pixel density of the camera by reading the manual, and calculate the shooting distance Y of the camera. In the actual operation, the focal length F and pixel density PPI of the camera are not need in this scheme. This is because the focal length of the manual is not equal to the actual focal length of the shot, and after the shot, the image collector software will also do some processing on the picture, resulting in a certain deviation between the reference parameters and the actual. In this scheme, the calibration method is used to avoid the problems caused by inaccurate camera parameters [11]. The detailed process is as follows:

Set the actual length of the QR-Code as X, and after shooting at the distance of Y_1 and Y_2, calculate the QR-Code pixels as X_1, X_2 respectively. K is the conversion coefficient from QR-Code pixel to cm. Rewrite Eq. 7 as follows:

$$Y_1 = F \frac{X}{KX_1} \tag{9}$$

$$Y_2 = F \frac{X}{KX_2} \tag{10}$$

Then, when a set of real value Y_2 is measured in advance, for any Y_1, it has:

$$\frac{Y_1}{Y_2} = \frac{X_2}{X_1} \tag{11}$$

After transformation, it has the following relations:

$$Y_1 = Y_2 \frac{X_2}{X_1} \tag{12}$$

The measured Y_1 is the straight-line distance from the QR-Code center point to the camera connection. In practice, the right edge of the left and right QR-Codes is used for distance measurement. Finally, take the average value of the two as the final result of measurement.

Angle Measurement. The system uses the rewritten MUSIC algorithm to calculate the camera's offset angle [12], and then deduces the actual offset distance DX, DY between the camera and the electronic screen. The calculation process is as follows.

After locating the left and right QR-Code areas, make four horizontal vertical tangents on the left and right QR-Code areas, and measure the distance of these four tangents as X1, X2, X3, X4 by distance measurement. At the same time, four vertical tangents of equal distance are made on the left and right QR-Code areas. The distance measured by the method of distance measurement is Y1, Y2, Y3, Y4. When the camera is horizontally deflected, the line deformation in the vertical direction is large, which is suitable for yaw angle estimation. Therefore, the data of Y1, Y2, Y3, Y4 are used for horizontal deflection angle measurement.

Similarly, X1, X2, X3, X4 data are used to estimate the pitch angle in the vertical direction.

Taking the horizontal deflection angle estimation as an example, the specific algorithm steps are as follows:

Set the tangent distance in the vertical direction is D, the incident signal is constructed:

$$X(i) = \begin{bmatrix} e^{z1} \\ e^{z2} \\ e^{z3} \\ e^{z4} \end{bmatrix} \tag{13}$$

$$z_1 = 0$$
$$z_2 = -2d\pi i \frac{Y_2 - Y_1}{d}$$
$$z_3 = -4d\pi i \frac{Y_3 - Y_2}{d}$$
$$z_4 = -6d\pi i \frac{Y_4 - Y_3}{d}$$

The covariance matrix of the input signal is calculated as follows:

$$R_x(i) = X(i)X^H(i) \tag{14}$$

H means the conjugate transpose of the matrix.

Eigen-Decomposition the covariance matrix obtained from the above:

$$R(i) = AR_x A^H + \sigma^2 I \tag{15}$$

σ^2 is the noise power and I is the unit matrix. The eigenvector corresponding to the eigenvalue γ is $V(\theta)$. Sorting the eigenvalues, the eigenvector corresponding to the largest eigenvalue is regarded as the signal, and the remaining three eigenvalues and eigenvectors are regarded as the noise. Get noise matrix E_n:

$$A^H v_i(\theta) = 0, i = 2, 3, 4$$
$$E_n = [v_2(\theta), v_3(\theta), v_4(\theta)] \tag{16}$$

The final estimated angle P is:

$$P = \frac{1}{\alpha^H(\theta) E_n E_n{}^H \alpha(\theta)} \tag{17}$$

4   Experimental Results

The principal objective of the experimental setup is to determine the accuracy of the proposed localization algorithm. The system uses a 55 in. large electronic screen with two QR-Codes arranged on the left and right of the electronic screen. The side length of the QR-Code is 488 mm, and the spacing between the two QR-Codes is 131 mm. In this scheme, image acquisition is carried out at different distances and angles to simulate robot positioning at different positions. The specific location is shown in Fig. 12.

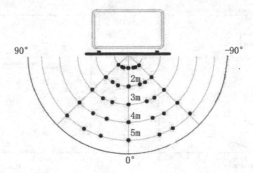

Fig. 12. Experiment layout, there are seven angle gradients (0, 11.31, 18.43, 21.8, 30.96, 45, 56.31) in the selected area. Some values (11.31, 21.8, 56.31) are not drawn in the figure.

Figure 13 shows the average error and RMSE between the estimated distance and the real distance of the system under different distances. The statistical data are taken in the central area. The statistical results show that the ranging errors of the system are all within 10 mm at a distance of 2–3 m, and increase with the increase of the distance. The ranging errors are also within 50 mm at a distance of 5 m, and the ranging accuracy of the whole system is high.

Some of the factors contributing to the location estimation errors are explained as follows. One of the main reasons is that there are some errors in the calculation of the actual pixels of QR-Code. The pixel length of QR-Code is small in long distance, and the pixel error when calculating the pixel side length of QR-Code has great influence on the calculation result.

It can be seen from the figure that when the deflection angle is 0°, the ranging error of the system is within 5 mm. The error of distance measurement increases with the increase of deflection angle. When the deflection angle is more than ±20°, the whole image can only be acquired through the deflection camera. At this time, because the deflection camera takes pictures, the line segment has a certain scale, so a new measurement error is introduced. Moreover, with the increase of camera deflection angle, the scaling ratio of line segment also increases, and the error also increases. In this scheme, the average value is used to reduce the new error, that is, the length of the line segment is cut off at different positions of the QR-Code to find the distance, and the average value of the distance is calculated as the final estimate value.

In addition, in the common methods of camera ranging, there is also the way of image comparison to ranging. We use SIFT algorithm in OpenCV to extract QR-Ccode for ranging [13] as a comparison with this scheme. The results of the distance measurement are shown in Fig. 13 and Fig. 14. It can be seen from the results that the ranging accuracy of this scheme is much higher than that of using image contrast method. This is because QR-Code is used as the location mark, which not only reduces the difficulty of image processing, but also does

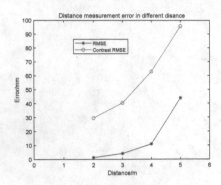
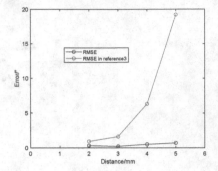

Fig. 13. RMSE of distance measurement errors at different distances

Fig. 14. RMSE of angle measurement errors at different angles

not depend on the accuracy of image contrast algorithm, thus greatly improving the accuracy of ranging.

The error results of angle measurement are shown in Fig. 14. As can be seen from the figure, the angle measurement results of this scheme are very accurate. MUSIC algorithm is introduced to enlarge the range of location, and the error of angle estimation is limited to 5°.

In the field of visible light screen communication positioning, we found another similar location scheme. In the paper of [14] mentions a similar positioning method, which uses the QR-Code pasted on the ceiling to carry out the precise positioning of indoor robot. In that scheme, the height of the ceiling corresponds to the distance in this scheme, which is a known parameter. In that scheme, the camera on the mobile robot collects the QR-Code image on the ceiling to calculate the two-dimensional coordinates of the robot relative to the QR-Code on the horizontal plane, and then calculate the actual position of the robot according to the absolute coordinates resolved in the QR-Code.

We use matlab to reproduce the positioning method in this paper. Then using this method, the coordinate distance between the image collector and the QR-Code is calculated. At last, we convert the result of calculation into the angle value.

As it can be seen from Fig. 14, in the central region, although the accuracy of the angle value calculated by that method is not as accurate as that calculated by this scheme, it still has a high quality calculation accuracy. But in the noncentral region, the angle error calculated by that method is very large. This also shows that method has some limitations, that is the location area can only be near the QR-Code but not too far away from the QR-Code. The method mentioned in this scheme has expanded the localization area and still increases localization accuracy.

As can be seen from the results, the localization error increases with the increase of distance and angle. In general the error depends on a number of factors, including the actual calibration of the true locations of the QR-Codes, as well as the edge distortion of camera in image acquisition. The camera with small distortion or camera calibration can be used to reduce the error [15]. Experimental results show that the localization can be achieved with reasonably good accuracy using the proposed localization method.

5   Conclusion

In the field of automatic driving, vehicle localization has been one of the challenging problems [16]. Accurate position information of a mobile robot is the foundation of automatic driving. This paper proposed an approach for vehicle localization using artificial landmarks made up of an electric card with two QR-Code on it. Image processing techniques, camera ranging technology and music algorithm are used to calculate the distance and angle of the robot. From repeated experimental tests the proposed method was able to achieve average localization accuracy with errors in the range 0 cm to 8 cm and angle errors is up to $\pm 5°$ in the location area with a distance of 5 m and a viewing angle range of $\pm 120°$. The overall results of the proposed method are found to be satisfactory for robot localization.

In future work, we plan to extend this work to further improve performance of the localization when the robot in long distance and large angle.

Acknowledgment. This work is supported by the Science and Technology Development Fund of Macao S.A.R (FDCT) under number 0015/2019/AKP, Guangdong Research Program (No. 2018B050502009), and Shenzhen Research Program (No. XMHT20190101035, JCYJ20170818153518789, KCXFZ20201221173613035).

References

1. Se, S., Lowe, D.G., Little, J.: Vision-based global localization and mapping for mobile robots. Proc. IEEE Trans. Robot. **21**, 217–226 (2005)
2. Kim, Y.-G., An, J., Lee, K.-D.: Localization of mobile robot based on fusion of artificial landmark and RF TDOA distance under indoor sensor network. Int. J. Adv. Robot. Syst. **8**(4), 203–211 (2011)
3. Priyantha, N.B.: The cricket indoor location system. Ph.D. thesis, Massachusetts Institute of Technology, June 2005
4. Tang, Z., Grompone von Gioi, R., Monasse, P., Morel, J.: A precision analysis of camera distortion models. IEEE Trans. Image Process. **26**(6), 2694–2704 (2017). https://doi.org/10.1109/TIP.2017.2686001
5. Qu, Z., Zhang, L.: Research on image segmentation based on the improved Otsu algorithm. In: 2010 Second International Conference on Intelligent Human-Machine Systems and Cybernetics, pp. 228–231 (2010). https://doi.org/10.1109/IHMSC.2010.157
6. Maragos, P.: Differential morphology and image processing. IEEE Trans. Image Process. **5**(6), 922–937 (1996). https://doi.org/10.1109/83.503909
7. Sonka, M., Hlavac, V., Boyle, R.: Image Processing, Analysis, and Machine Vision, 2nd edn. People Post Press, Beijing (2001)

8. Garateguy, G.J., Arce, G.R., Lau, D.L., Villarreal, O.P.: QR images: optimized image embedding in QR codes. IEEE Trans. Image Process. **23**(7), 2842–2853 (2014). https://doi.org/10.1109/TIP.2014.2321501
9. Yuan, T., Wang, Y., Xu, K., Martin, R.R., Hu, S.: Two-layer QR codes. IEEE Trans. Image Process. **28**(9), 4413–4428 (2019). https://doi.org/10.1109/TIP.2019.2908490
10. Dandil, E., Çevİk, K.K.: Computer vision based distance measurement system using stereo camera view. In: 2019 3rd International Symposium on Multidisciplinary Studies and Innovative Technologies (ISMSIT), pp. 1–4 (2019). https://doi.org/10.1109/ISMSIT.2019.8932817
11. Taketomi, T., Okada, K., Yamamoto, G., Miyazaki, J., Kato, H.: Geometric registration for zoomable camera using epipolar constraint and pre-calibrated intrinsic camera parameter change. In: 2013 IEEE International Symposium on Mixed and Augmented Reality (ISMAR), pp. 295–296 (2013). https://doi.org/10.1109/ISMAR.2013.6671812
12. Gupta, P., Kar, S.P.: MUSIC and improved MUSIC algorithm to estimate direction of arrival. In: 2015 International Conference on Communications and Signal Processing (ICCSP), pp. 0757–0761 (2015). https://doi.org/10.1109/ICCSP.2015.7322593
13. Han, Y., Zhang, Z., Dai, M.: Monocular vision system for distance measurement based on feature points. Opt. Precis. Eng. **19**(005), 1110–1117 (2011)
14. Lee, S.-J., Tewolde, G., Lim, J., Kwon, J.: QR-code based Localization for Indoor Mobile Robot with validation using a 3D optical tracking instrument. In: 2015 IEEE International Conference on Advanced Intelligent Mechatronics (AIM), Busan, Korea. IEEE (2015)
15. Torres, J., Menendez, J.M.: A practical algorithm to correct geometrical distortion of image acquisition cameras. In: 2004 International Conference on Image Processing, ICIP 2004, vol. 4, pp. 2451–2454 (2004). https://doi.org/10.1109/ICIP.2004.1421598
16. Lin, M., Yoon, J., Kim, B.: Self-driving car location estimation based on a particle-aided unscented Kalman filter. Sensors **20**(9), 2544 (2020)

BBServerless: A Bursty Traffic Benchmark for Serverless

Yanying Lin[1,2], Kejiang Ye[1](✉), Yongkang Li[1,2], Peng Lin[1,2], Yingfei Tang[3], and Chengzhong Xu[4]

[1] Guangdong-Hong Kong-Macao Joint Laboratory of Human-Machine
Intelligence-Synergy Systems, Shenzhen Institute of Advanced Technology,
Chinese Academy of Sciences, Shenzhen 518055, China
{yy.lin1,kj.ye,yk.li1,peng.lin}@siat.ac.cn
[2] University of Chinese Academy of Sciences, Beijing 100049, China
[3] Ping An Insurance Company of China, Ltd., Shenzhen 518055, China
[4] State Key Lab of IoTSC, Faculty of Science and Technology, University of Macau,
Macau SAR, China
czxu@um.edu.mo

Abstract. Serverless is a mainstream computing mode in modern cloud native systems. Different from traditional monolithic cloud, workloads for Serverless architecture are disaggregated into short-lived and fine-grained functions. In Serverless, functions are usually invoked with a *bursty* pattern, which means the system needs to deliver these functions at high throughput to meet SLA (Service-level agreement) requirements. To explore bursty traffic implications on Serverless platforms, in this paper, we propose a novel benchmarking suite for serverless systems - **BBServerless**. BBServerless is designed to capture end-to-end and system-level performance in bursty-traffic workloads which help reveal performance bottlenecks of Serverless platform and guide better architecture design for cloud systems. To demonstrate performance variations on Serverless platforms, we also design a traffic generating algorithm (based on *Poisson distribution*) for four mainstream cloud workloads, i.e. Big-Data, Stream processing (STREAM), Web Applications (WebApps), and Machine Learning Inference (MaLI). We conduct experiments with trace-driven simulations in a private cloud environment. With data collected from evaluations, we observe that the performance of time-localized components like CPU migration, branch prediction, and cache is highly correlated with end-to-end workload performance. and publicly available at Github (https://github.com/whoszus/BurstyServerlessBenchmark).

Keywords: Serverless computing · Bursty traffic · Architectural analytics · Benchmark suit · Serverless workloads

1 Introduction

Serverless computing is a new paradigm for cloud computing that creatively shifts cloud services from monolithic applications to short-lived and fine-grained

© Springer Nature Switzerland AG 2022
K. Ye and L.-J. Zhang (Eds.): CLOUD 2021, LNCS 12989, pp. 45–60, 2022.
https://doi.org/10.1007/978-3-030-96326-2_4

functions. In Serverless, cloud platforms manage the provisioning of services in a transparent, auto-scaling manner without developers involved. Developers are charged on a pay-per-use pricing model, proportional to the resources provided and used per request, with no fees levied when the service is idle.

Serverless computing quickly gained popularity in the cloud market because it is a way to run stateless, easily scalable, developer-operations-free cloud services that reduce user costs. Serverless functions are event-driven and are invoked by user-initiated HTTP requests or triggered by functions on invocation chains. To match the invocation traffic and improve platform-wide *Throughput* of services, Serverless automatically scales resources horizontally available to run more instances of the invoked function in parallel. Resources are automatically reclaimed by the platform for a short period (warm-up period) after function idle, which is called *short-lived lifecycle*. In addition, concurrency of invocation also increased since Serverless disaggregated application to fine-grained functions. Consequently, Serverless platform needs to rapidly manage resources and response invocations in high throughput, which result in workloads corresponded with *bursty* patterns.

Bursty traffic is an extreme case of highly concurrent invocations, generally leading to SLO violations [6,11,18]; however, it is not a highlighted problem for cloud platforms serving traditional service workloads such as monolithic applications and microservices. Long-running microservices usually reserved excessive resources and therefore can provide services at a high percentage of parallelism and concurrency to circumvent **cold start** [21]. For instance, Java microservices are usually allocated more than 4 cores of CPU and 512 MB of memory, which can cope with concurrency HTTP invocations by forking and pooling multiple threads with low overheads [8,13,15–17,22]. Moreover, microservices can communicate through memory sharing between threads, relieving the system load encountering concurrency invocations. Nevertheless, to cope with traffic bursts, users, and cloud providers have both paid extra monetary costs; microservices need to pay for idle resources, and cloud providers, on the other hand, are expected to be financially savvy to harvest idle resources from customer virtual machine to achieve high utilization of resources (i.e., over commit) [1,3,4,25].

Serverless provides automated and transparent resource management by designing innovative frameworks and feature-compliant scheduling policies to escape the dilemma of inadequate resource allocation elasticity. But meanwhile, these features make for a highly dynamic system that brings new, unforeseen overheads and challenges for platform designing and optimization, e.g. longer queue times, competition for resources between instances. To meet the SLAs (Service-Level Agreements) of services in bursty-traffic workloads, a low-load Serverless platform needs to finish a series of tasks such as resource allocation and runtime preparation within milliseconds. However, the current strategies are not designed to accommodate low latency requirements, which jeopardized the prior wisdom of performance optimization for cloud computing.

To investigate the bursty-traffic implications on Serverless platform, in this work, we present a benchmarking suite, **BBServerless**, to precisely control invocation traffic using an algorithm based on *Poisson distribution*. BBServerless is designed to capture multidimensional performance metrics including end-to-end level, e.g., *Throughput, Response Time, Failure Rate, etc.* and system-level, e.g., *CPU Migration, Context Switch, LLC Cache misses, etc.* In addition, to investigate performance of difference application, BBServerless provides four types of workloads including BigData, Stream processing (STREAM), Web Applications (WebApps), and Machine Learning Inference (MaLI) based on characteristics derived from Microsoft and Google cluster traces [1,14,26]. The main contributions of this paper are as follows:

C1. We argue that bursty traffic is a key feature that jeopardizes the performance of Serverless platforms.
C2. We designed and open-sourced BBServerless, a new Serverless benchmark for bursty traffic, enabling cloud platform designers to use representative platforms for architecture design simulation and analysis.
C3. We provide multidimensional system-level performance metrics and their correlation with end-to-end performance analysis.

2 Background and Related Work

Early work in Serverless analytics has identified the challenges of platforms coping with bursty traffic. We build on our study of bursty traffic for Serverless representative architectures to investigate the fundamental properties of a platform that supports high throughput. Our focus is to explore what architecture has the potential to support high concurrency while avoiding SLO violations, since Serverless is a highly dynamic distributed system with a complex way of structuring components and varying degrees of dependence on cloud infrastructure.

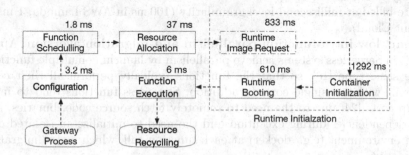

Fig. 1. Overhead and execution processing of hello world function in OpenWhisk. Runtime initialization could be a skipable phase in warming-up running patterns. Function execution phase has low percentage of overhead.

2.1   Serverless Function Invocations

The invocation of Serverless functions consists of two phases: function programming and invoking. Serverless developers start with developing and configuring functions with the rules of the platform provided and get invocation URLs for users. These functions (including function code, invocation dependencies, and initialization configurations) will be stored in the cluster middlewares, such as CouchDB, Redis. To ensure efficient access to data, Serverless platforms commonly use memory-based caching middleware [12].

Functions invoked by calling URLs or periodic triggers with events configured by the developer. To meet SLA requirements, the Serverless platform needs to schedule function instances and orchestrate running environments (containers and function runtimes) in high throughput, which may introduce challenges for cloud platforms. The function would be recycling by platform configured policies, in process of *ready, running, pre-warming, and deleted*. Instances of functions would be automatically scaling (both out or down) by Serverless platform, which presented an ultimate pay-as-you-go features for users.

2.2   Characteristics of Serverless Functions

Serverless computing introduces several very new characteristics. First, functions usually run in **stateless** that intermediate data (i.e., state) is usually stored outside the hosted container (e.g., in a database [10]). Stateless creates a good architecture for horizontal scaling that new instances can parallel executing functions only needs to access these states by the HTTP request.

Second, **lightweight**, which is reflected in two aspects, code and executing time. Developers can reduce the amount of code required to write and focus on unique application logic, while all other issues are supported by cloud-provided and managed cloud services. According to the analysis of real-world Serverless workloads [5,19], 82% of use cases consist of 5 or fewer functions; functions typically living in the range of a few hundred milliseconds to a few minutes and are billed at millisecond-level granularity (100 ms in AWS Lambda, 1 ms in Tencent Cloud).

Third, **low intra-function parallelism and migration aversion**. Applications in Serverless systems achieve parallelism by launching multiple functions at the same time [10], so that the functions typically perform all their computations within a single core. In addition, Serverless functions tend to incur startup costs [24] due to the need to remotely fetch source code, binaries, and other dependencies during execution and the need to initialize an isolated execution environment (e.g., docker) at each function call, which makes migration unattractive.

Last, services be disaggregated into fine-grained Serverless functions, increasing the number of invocations and the complexity of collaborating for a single action. For instance, user login may need to invoke 3 or more functions in Serverless. Numerous simultaneously requested functions and complex invocation relationships (e.g., triggers and invocation chain) highlighted **bursty traffic** in the whole picture of Serverless characteristics. *We observed that traditional strategies restricted by the concept of optimizing resources jeopardized end-to-end performances of functions, like response time, Transactions Per Second (TPS), and throughput.* Fine-grained executing units also introduce new SLA requirements, like more strict response time constraints. Consequently, Serverless demands a more aggressive resource management strategy compared to traditional cloud services. Previous studies have stated series of investigations for this problem:

$\mathcal{E}$1. Studies [7,9] investigated real-world workloads in AWS and Azure, which showed that the parallelism level of Serverless functions can fluctuate by several orders of magnitude in a few seconds.

$\mathcal{E}$2. S. Eismann, et al. [5] tested workloads on a Serverless platform to determine if the functionality maintains high volatility.

$\mathcal{E}$3. 81% of the workload patterns of those tested were burst, indicating that burst is a common and essential characteristic of Serverless computing.

Such a large percentage of bursty traffic demonstrates the urgency and necessity of our research.

3   The BBServerless Benchmark Design

BBServerless uses four representative Serverless applications and proposes five monitoring metrics, as shown in Fig. 1 BBServerless is designed to characterize the performance of Serverless platforms and help reveal the performance shortcomings of different platforms under bursty traffic scenarios to inspire the program and architecture design of Serverless.

3.1   Principles

BBServerless is designed to comply with open-source and high availability principles. In this work, we mainly use three mainstream open-source Serverless platforms as reference targets. Due to the short lifecycle nature of Serverless, it is extremely sensitive to the request time of the load. Differences in design function code and small differences in load initiation time can produce performance differences. Therefore, we follow the following principles when implementing Benchmark:

$\mathcal{P}$1: **Fairness.** Serverless platforms differ in system architecture, such as the middleware used, function invocation procedures, and runtime environments. To avoid performance differences due to system configuration, we customized the container image using the platform's default language runtime environment, e.g., using *OpenWhisk/python3action:nightly* to build the OpenWhisk python3-based function containers. We also conducted experiments in cluster infrastructures with the same server configuration, network bandwidth, and basic platform (e.g., Kubernetes).

$\mathcal{P}$2: **Stateless.** All functions proposed in BBServerless run stateless. The function of Serverless usually run in containers which would be recycling while function exit. Consequently, the application state (i.e., intermediate data produced during the execution) is stored in a database outside the hosted container and be fetched by a new instance in needed [10]. Although state-based services may face network overhead, in bursty traffic, stateless would be a performance booster for platform resource management, as well as end-to-end performances. Some works have discussed and addressed it by proposing stateful Serverless computing [2,20,23], but, resource overhead is uncontrollable and violates the principle of fairness.

$\mathcal{P}$3: **Relevance.** We carefully examine Serverless use cases in the literature to select representative workloads that emphasize different performance metrics for Serverless platforms. We are focused on *architectures implications* and expect to remain relevant for the foreseeable future.

Table 1. Function execution time and memory overhead. **TC** denotes Text Classify, **IC** denotes Images Classify.

Category	Functions (Task)	Exec. (ms)	MEM. (MB)	Description
Web applications	Hello	7	99.22	Receive parameters and return function results using json.dumps()
	Hash	6	67.3	
	Sort	6	75.72	
	MD5	8	101.72	
	Cryptography	40	141.41	
ML inference	PGclassifier (**TC**)	394	287.28	P: Load model using HTTP, and proceed inference task
	sgdregressor (**IC**)	479	288.16	
	sgdclassifier (**TC**)	477	288.53	
	perceptron (**IC**)	480	287.28	
	faceRecognition	658	287.59	
	svr (**IC**)	2306	286.13	
	multinomialnb (**TC**)	377	287.78	
	RFgressor (**TC**)	780	288.09	
BigData	Bigdata	**6598**	492.09	Word counting (128 MB)
Stream	Stream	34	216.78	Word counting (random)

3.2   Web Applications (WebAPPS)

Web services represent lightweight workloads in cloud. Similarly, in Serverless, web services applications are lightweight in terms of code and execution overheads. Firstly, functions of web services are usually logical operations (e.g. if-else), so the execution time of functions usually within 5 ms (e.g. function hello life cycle, as shown in Fig. 1) to 1 s. Secondly, web services are very much in line with the localization principle. From the spatial perspective, only a few functions are called frequently, and 10% of them can cope with nearly 95% of the traffic, which shows sufficient spatial locality nature. From the request time aspect, web services usually have periodic request peaks. For instance, requests for online taxi services commonly burst during rush hours and moderate at work hours, which reveals temporal locality nature.

To investigate the bursty performance of the Serverless platform, BBServerless disaggregated an authorization microservice into lightweight functions sets. Specifically, we constructed five Serverless functions based on the authorization microservice components: cookie authentication (*Hash calculation*), username password encryption and decryption (*encryption and decryption*), account password authentication (*MD5*), last login time (*sorting algorithm*), and login result processing (*hello function*). The execution time and memory overhead of the functions are shown in the Table 1, which are inline of serverless function characteristics mentioned above. To reveal the programming languages implications, Web Applications of BBServerless also support mainstream languages e.g., Python, JavaScript, Go, and Java etc.

3.3 BigData Processing (BigData)

Big data processing refers to technical architectures, analytical tools that meet scale, distribution, diversity, and timeliness metrics in order to gain insights that can unlock new sources of business value. There are currently two main forms of BigData: offline data and real-time data (also known as streaming data). Streaming data is data that is continuously generated from thousands of data sources, often also sent simultaneously as data records, and processed at a smaller scale in a single session. For example, the Google Maps navigation function that collects GPS signals (latitude, longitude, or location codes) and then plans a route is real-time streaming data, updated in real-time and always changing. Whereas the data processed by BigData is usually historical; Google Maps, for example, the GPS data of a city in the past year is a kind of offline data that can be used to analyze the travel preferences of the residents of this city, etc. The pay-as-you-go nature of Serverless is a cost-effective property for BigData. In Big Data, dynamic scaling and cost management are key factors in the success of any platform. Serverless cloud computing enables self-service configuration and management of servers, effectively reducing costs.

BBServerless implements a word counting function with a text size of 128 MB (consistent with the default block size of HDFS) and is stored in the container image. BigData functions typically have greater overhead, including more CPU requiring and memory footprint, and longer execution times, as shown in Table 1. Studying the performance of the BigData function in a Serverless platform can help reveal insight for programming and architectural designing.

3.4 Streaming Data Processing (STREAM)

Similar to Web services, streaming data processing is a relatively lightweight application that is typically used to process logs or mathematical operations, such as analyzing keywords in logs or performing statistics. Developers use streaming to query a continuous stream of data and react to important events and rank them in a short time frame (from milliseconds to minutes). Much of the streaming data is received in real-time and is most valuable as it arrives. For example, a social network may want to detect trending topics within minutes, and an operator may want to detect a failure within seconds. Because of its inherent statelessness, lightweight and scalability, industry and academia have begun to explore the application of Serverless computing to streaming data processing.

Stream processing is closely related to real-time analytics, complex event processing, and stream analysis. Streaming data processing applications typically acquire data over the network, and the amount of data processed in a single session is typically small (from 1 KB to several MB), resulting in relatively short execution times. In addition, streaming data arrives continuously, so proper runtime reservation and warming up would potentially improve the performances of streaming processing. Its bursty traffic effect is also more significant compared to other categories of applications.

BBServerless is designed with streaming word counting and hot word sorting functions. According to the characteristics of stream data processing, the function call first obtains text data through an HTTP request, then counts and sorts it, and finally returns the result to end the function execution. BBServerless investigates the performance of stream data processing on Serverless computing through different traffic policies, to explore the performance differences of platform architectures in dealing with burst stream data requests to reveal architecture design and scheduling strategy research.

3.5   Machine Learning Inferences (MaLI)

The widespread adoption of machine learning techniques in a wide range of domains such as image recognition, speech and text processing has made machine learning one of the most widely used workloads in cloud services today. Serverless has become a popular architecture as far as serving model inference is concerned. The majority of ML deployments can be conceptualized as a simple *predict*(). From a developer's perspective, it is meaningful to deploy a model on a Serverless computing platform such as OpenFaas if the model is essentially just a function. From the application characteristics, machine learning inference is well suited for Serverless computing. Models for ML usually have specific tasks, so encapsulating the model into a function usually requires no interaction between functions and is highly isolated, enabling easy function scaling. Function parallelism is achieved through a reasonable scaling strategy provided by the platform to accommodate bursty traffic.

While there is no container instance scaling concerns, latency in an invocation of machine learning functions is a challenge that Serverless platforms are facing. First, runtime initialization latency. Machine learning models are typically stored in containers (e.g., Docker images) after training is complete, resulting in large container images that require more time to fetch images from the network and load them from the disk. In addition, before executing the function, not only perform the machine learning libraries (e.g., *Scikit* or *PyTorch* for python) have to be loaded, but also the model has to be loaded into memory, resulting in a large cold-start overhead. Therefore, how to reduce invocation latency, e.g., a proper configuration of function runtime reservation and preheating policies will be a key factor for platform performance under bursty traffic. Second, it will be a challenge for the existing platform to arrange intra-function and inter-function parallelism and overall resource scheduling in the case of bursty traffic.

BBServerless pre-trained 8 machine learning algorithms and conduct their standard applications, such as *SGDClassifier* for text classification and SVC for image recognition. Functions in BBServerless represents mainstream machine learning workloads to cloud computing. BBServerless explores the performance of the Serverless platform in terms of resource allocation and task management in scheduling machine learning inferences and complex loads with a mixture of machine learning inferences through different traffic bursting strategies to inspire the design of Serverless architecture and resource allocation policies.

4   Traffic Patterns

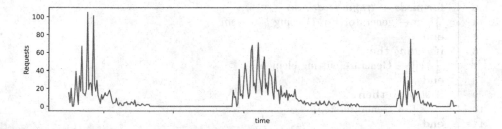

Fig. 2. Three presented traffic patterns of BBServerless.

Traffic bursting patterns are a key element in studying the performance of Serverless platforms. However, to our knowledge, there is no precise definition and related research on bursty traffic patterns, especially for Serverless computing. In this work, we introduce a traffic pattern consistent with *Poisson distribution* with manual modulate the open-source Serverless platforms, as shown in the following:

$$M_X(t) = E\left[e^{tX}\right] = \sum_{x=0}^{\infty} e^{tx}\frac{e^{-\lambda}\lambda^x}{x!} = e^{-\lambda}\sum_{x=0}^{\infty}\frac{(e^t\lambda)^x}{x!} = e^{\lambda(e^t-1)} \tag{1}$$

Characteristics of workload for different categories of applications are usually inconsistent. For instance, Big data processing requires long runtimes and low invocation frequencies, while Web services are invoked frequently but have runtimes as short as milliseconds. Therefore, it is not practical enough to measure the performance of applications and platforms using workloads built with the same traffic patterns. A more reasonable way is to customize the traffic patterns according to the characteristics of the application. We construct the traffic request stack using Algorithm 1, as shown in Fig. 2.

BBServerless designs two traffic patterns to evaluate the performance of Serverless platforms, single-category (e.g., using web services alone) and hybrid mode. Real-world workloads are also referenced [19] to optimize the traffic bursty patterns. Preliminary experiments were proposed in tiny cloud clusters to clip the bursty-traffic load X of the Serverless platform. In a cluster with 3 nodes, OpenWhisk has a single machine load of 180 applications such as web services (with a failure rate of less than 1% as measured by the tools provided in the suite). Taking into account the characteristics of different kinds of functions, BBServerless provides configurable bursty traffic levels.

Algorithm 1: traffic generation

---

   input : workloads steps s, and params t for Eq. 1
   output: w: a workload matrix

1   *params initialization:* $w \leftarrow []$;
2   **for** $p \leftarrow platforms$ **do**
3   **for** $mode \leftarrow traffic\ modes$ **do**
4 | $m \leftarrow$ generator(Eq. 1) using t $w \leftarrow m$
5   **end**
6   **if** *cutting* **then**
7 | $c[] \leftarrow$ Generate(cutting element)
8   **end**
9   **if** *step ¿ s* **then**
10 | $s[] \leftarrow$ Generate(step)
11   **end**
12 **end**
13 **foreach** *element e of w, c, s* **do** CuttingWorkload(e);

---

5   Platforms Performance with Bursty Traffic

In this work, we conduct experiments in a local cloud environment with 39 servers, named SIAT Cloud. To reveal platform performances in a small cluster, we also config a tiny cluster with 3 servers tagged, which include a Kubernetes master node and 2 worker nodes. All reported performance data are collected from the tiny cluster. Servers are homogeneous, which contains 32 core Intel Xeon CPU E5-2630 v3, 64 GB RAM, and 1 GB network bandwidth.

5.1   Response Time

Function Response Time (RT) is a widely-used metric, which provides a direct indicator of system performance. To meet SLA requirements, Serverless

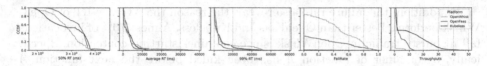

Fig. 3. The end-to-end metrics CCDF (Eq. 2) of OpenWhisk, OpenFaas and Kubeless, under the workload of Fig. 2.

platforms will endure a complicated period of task scheduling and resource management patterns. Fine-grained performance parameters help users and platforms to judge the execution situation. However, the user could not get a glimpse of specific execution details, and the most intuitive manifestation of the function running is HTTP state pending. The tools for cloud providers and service users to analyze function end-to-end metrics are a scarcity.

To give a detailed report of function running statistics, BBServerless offers Average RT, 50% RT, 75% RT, 95% RT, and 99% RT. In this work, we perf the response time of OpenWhisk, OpenFaas, and Kubeless using the traffic generated by Sect. 4, as shown in Fig. 3. We use CCDF, formulated as follows, to illustrate the distribution of response time.

$$F_X(x) = P(X \geq x) \tag{2}$$

OpenWhisk introduces more efficiency in executing functions, as shown in 50% RT, most of the functions are completed faster than OpenFaas and Kubeless. However, in 99% RT as well as Average RT, the OpenWhisk function performs a lower mathematical expectation. These three figures indicate that Open-Whisk presents tail-latency performances in response time which may lead to the conclusion of insufficient stability.

5.2 Failure Rate

To study the stability of Serverless platforms and reveal the response time implications, we present new metrics to illustrate the SLO violations, named failure rate. A high failure rate function jeopardizes the whole system performance, which needs to invoke the task again that raising function response time and wasting user budgets. Functions may experience OOM (Out of memory), timeouts, code uncached exceptions, etc., and thus terminate their life cycle prematurely, which we capture as a failure.

As shown in Fig. 3, OpenWhisk introduced a high percentage of failure, and Kubeless showed none in the same pattern of request traffic. The Open-Whisk platform use non-parallelism strategies in function scheduling, which leads to cold-starting up a bunch of containers to handle bursty invocations. Non-parallelism policy is a nature of Serverless functions in the above analytics (Sect. 2), however, we observe that parallelism in individual function instances (i.e. container) would help to reduce network and cold start stress.

In addition, the failure rate also reveals the reason the Average RT of Open-Whisk performs better than OpenFaas and Kubeless. Almost 70% of invocations fail in bursty traffic in OpenWhisk, since container starting contention. Specifically, a container of function A has been killed before the next function A invocation arrives by the platform, releasing resources to handle other requests. We propose that a function moderated replacement policies in resource-limited scenarios would promote the system performances by decreasing the failure rate.

5.3 Throughput

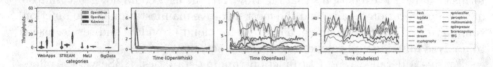

Fig. 4. The throughput (TP) of functions. Sub-figure 1 demonstrates the categories TP distributions, which shows that Kubeless has better TP of all kind of workload. Sub-figure 2–4 illustrates the TP of all functions in evaluated platforms respectively.

Another metric of cloud systems to describe the overall performance of platforms is throughput. Throughput generally presents two pros: intuitive means of function performance statistics and indirect platform performance. BBServerless introduces a detailed throughput report including function throughput, invocation period throughput, and function categories throughput.

As shown in Fig. 3, Kubeless is the top-level throughput producer in three evaluated platforms. More fine-grained reports for function throughput are shown in Fig. 4, which illustrated an interesting result of the Serverless platform managing bursty invocations. Although the throughput of OpenFaas and Open-Whisk is lower than Kubeless, we observe that the top 3 throughput functions are inconsistent. In Kubeless, hash, bigdata and sort function are demonstrated with a throughput of 30–40 levels, while OpenFaas are md5, sort, and hello. Bigdata requires a large amount of CPU and memory resources, and as shown in Table 1, runs in the longest time of all proposed functions. We will discuss this problem in our future works.

We also observed that function throughput for MaLI (Machine Learning inference) for all platforms is the least level. Containers for MaLI are reconstructed using Dockerfiles, which installed the machine basic libs (e.g., pandas, Scikit, etc.) and mounted their trained algorithm models into containers. As demonstrated in Table 1, an individual Bigdata function runs in 6500 ms far exceeds MaLI functions. We will also discuss this problem in our future works.

5.4 System-Level Performance

To reveal system-level indicators for Serverless platforms, BBServerless presents a series of perf tools that collects system-level metrics, e.g., CPU migration counts, cache miss, context switching counts, etc. Small system-level variations can easily be amplified to end-to-end performance across the entire load, which has an impact on the stability as well as reliability of platforms. For example, CPU migration in NUMA architecture servers may cross the NUMA socket, which means cache miss, memory reloading, and stack refresh in the next round of function execution that consumes more CPU cycles. Analytics of system-level metrics proposed in BBServerless helps to investigate the implications of the architecture of the Serverless platform framework meeting bursty traffic.

We present four time-localized metrics, as illustrated in Fig. 5, we observed that OpenWhisk demonstrated poor localized management, which correlate with the end-to-end performance, calculated by the formula as follows:

$$\rho(X,Y) = \frac{E\left[(X-\mu_X)(Y-\mu_Y)\right]}{\sigma_X \sigma_Y} = \frac{E\left[(X-\mu_X)(Y-\mu_Y)\right]}{\sqrt{\sum_{i=1}^{n}(X_i-\mu_X)^2}\sqrt{\sum_{i=1}^{n}(Y_i-\mu_Y)^2}}$$

ρ denotes correlation coefficient; X, Y denote throughput and system-level performances respectively.

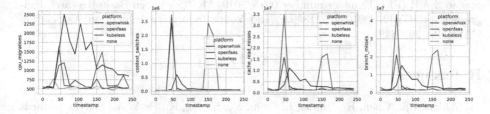

Fig. 5. Subset of system-level performance *perf* by BBServerless, including CPU migration, context switch, and branch prediction misses.

6   Discussion

Serverless architecture is designed and constructed to meet SLA requirements, which are represented as function response time and throughput. However, end-to-end level metrics are challenged to reveal platform bottlenecks. For instance, the function may migrate thousands of times while executing and demonstrated as a stall or several milliseconds of overhead in response time. In this case, system-level metrics fulfill this gap and present a way for programmer and architecture engineers to optimize the efficiency of functions. Nevertheless, system-level metrics are too much and too complicated, which may contain thousands of metrics and is a time-consuming task for us to dig out useful ones.

In this work, we used time-localized components as a cornerstone to understanding the architecture of mainstream open-sourced Serverless platforms. We observe that Kubeless performance is better than other platforms since the better time-localized policies are used, and OpenWhisk misses the branch prediction too many leads to poor performances. We also demonstrated the correlation coefficient of system-level and end-to-end level metrics to prove our hypothesis.

7   Conclusion

Serverless is becoming the established standard for cloud computing. However, the performance of Serverless is almost a black box for users in the mainstream platform, which jeopardized the optimization of code as well as platform architectures. To reveal architectural implications of Serverless workloads, in this work, we proposed BBServerless, a Benchmark suit for Serverless in bursty traffic. BBServerless presents end-to-end performance analytics, system-level performance analytics, and tools to collect data for it. We also introduce a traffic generation algorithm based on our understanding of cutting-edge commercial cloud workloads and conduct a series of experiments based on it. With data collected from evaluations, we observed that the performance of time-localized components like CPU migration, branch prediction, and cache highly correlated with end-to-end performance. BBServerless is open-sourced in Github[1].

Acknowledgment. This work is supported by Key-Area Research and Development Program of Guangdong Province (NO. 2020B010164003), National Natural Science Foundation of China (No. 62072451), Science and Technology Development Fund of Macao S.A.R (FDCT) under number 0015/2019/AKP, Shenzhen Basic Research Program (No. JCYJ20200109115418592), and Youth Innovation Promotion Association CAS (NO. 2019349).

References

1. Akkus, I.E., Chen, R., Rimac, I., Stein, M., Satzke, K., Beck, A.: SAND: towards high-performance serverless computing. In: ATC 2018, pp. 923–935 (2018)
2. Barcelona-Pons, D., Sánchez-Artigas, M., París, G., Sutra, P., García-López, P.: On the FaaS track: building stateful distributed applications with serverless architectures. In: Middleware 2019, pp. 41–54 (2019). https://doi.org/10.1145/3361525.3361535
3. Carver, B., Zhang, J., Wang, A., Anwar, A., Wu, P., Cheng, Y.: LADS: a high-performance framework for serverless parallel computing. In: Proceedings of the ACM Symposium on Cloud Computing, SoCC 2020. Association for Computing Machinery (2020)
4. Delimitrou, C., Kozyrakis, C.: Quasar: resource-efficient and QoS-aware cluster management. In: Proceedings of the 19th International Conference on Architectural Support for Programming Languages and Operating Systems, ASPLOS 2014, pp. 127–144. Association for Computing Machinery, New York (2014). https://doi.org/10.1145/2541940.2541941
5. Eismann, S., et al.: A review of serverless use cases and their characteristics. CoRR abs/2008.11110 (2020)
6. Ferguson, A.D., Bodik, P., Kandula, S., Boutin, E., Fonseca, R.: Jockey: guaranteed job latency in data parallel clusters. In: Proceedings of the 7th ACM European Conference on Computer Systems, EuroSys 2012, pp. 99–112. Association for Computing Machinery, New York (2012). https://doi.org/10.1145/2168836.2168847

---

[1] https://github.com/whoszus/BurstyServerlessBenchmark.

7. Fouladi, S., et al.: From laptop to lambda: outsourcing everyday jobs to thousands of transient functional containers. In: USENIX ATC 2019, pp. 475–488 (2019)
8. Gan, Y., Delimitrou, C.: The architectural implications of cloud microservices. IEEE Comput. Archit. Lett. **17**(2), 155–158 (2018)
9. Jonas, E., Pu, Q., Venkataraman, S., Stoica, I., Recht, B.: Occupy the cloud: distributed computing for the 99%. In: Proceedings of the 2017 Symposium on Cloud Computing, pp. 445–451 (2017)
10. Kaffes, K., Yadwadkar, N.J., Kozyrakis, C.: Centralized core-granular scheduling for serverless functions. In: Proceedings of the ACM Symposium on Cloud Computing, pp. 158–164 (2019)
11. Kalia, A., Kaminsky, M., Andersen, D.G.: FaSSt: fast, scalable and simple distributed transactions with two-sided (RDMA) datagram RPCs. In: 12th USENIX Symposium on Operating Systems Design and Implementation (OSDI 2016), pp. 185–201. USENIX Association, Savannah, November 2016
12. Klimovic, A., Wang, Y., Stuedi, P., Trivedi, A., Pfefferle, J., Kozyrakis, C.: Pocket: elastic ephemeral storage for serverless analytics. In: 13th USENIX Symposium on Operating Systems Design and Implementation (OSDI 2018), pp. 427–444. USENIX Association, Carlsbad, October 2018
13. Lee, H., Satyam, K., Fox, G.: Evaluation of production serverless computing environments. In: 2018 IEEE 11th International Conference on Cloud Computing (CLOUD), pp. 442–450. IEEE (2018)
14. Lu, C., Chen, W., Ye, K., Xu, C.Z.: Understanding the workload characteristics in alibaba: a view from directed acyclic graph analysis. In: 2020 International Conference on High Performance Big Data and Intelligent Systems (HPBD&IS), pp. 1–8. IEEE (2020)
15. Maissen, P., Felber, P., Kropf, P., Schiavoni, V.: FaaSdom: a benchmark suite for serverless computing. In: Proceedings of the 14th ACM International Conference on Distributed and Event-based Systems, pp. 73–84 (2020)
16. McGrath, G., Brenner, P.R.: Serverless computing: design, implementation, and performance. In: 2017 IEEE 37th International Conference on Distributed Computing Systems Workshops (ICDCSW), pp. 405–410. IEEE (2017)
17. Müller, I., Marroquín, R., Alonso, G.: Lambada: interactive data analytics on cold data using serverless cloud infrastructure. In: Lambada, SIGMOD 2020, pp. 115–130. Association for Computing Machinery (2020). https://doi.org/10.1145/3318464.3389758
18. Pu, Q., Venkataraman, S., Stoica, I.: Shuffling, fast and slow: scalable analytics on serverless infrastructure. In: 16th USENIX Symposium on Networked Systems Design and Implementation (NSDI 2019), pp. 193–206. USENIX Association, Boston, February 2019
19. Shahrad, M., et al.: Serverless in the wild: characterizing and optimizing the serverless workload at a large cloud provider. In: USENIX ATC 2020, pp. 205–218 (2020)
20. Shillaker, S., Pietzuch, P.: FAASM: lightweight isolation for efficient stateful serverless computing. In: 2020 USENIX Annual Technical Conference (USENIX ATC 2020), pp. 419–433. USENIX Association, July 2020
21. Silva, P., Fireman, D., Pereira, T.E.: Prebaking functions to warm the serverless cold start. In: Proceedings of the 21st International Middleware Conference, Middleware 2020, pp. 1–13. Association for Computing Machinery, New York (2020). https://doi.org/10.1145/3423211.3425682
22. Somu, N., Daw, N., Bellur, U., Kulkarni, P.: PanOpticon: a comprehensive benchmarking tool for serverless applications. In: 2020 International Conference on COMmunication Systems & NETworkS (COMSNETS), pp. 144–151. IEEE (2020)

23. Sreekanti, V., et al.: Cloudburst: stateful functions-as-a-service. Proc. VLDB Endow. **13**(11), 2438–2452 (2020)
24. Wang, L., Li, M., Zhang, Y., Ristenpart, T., Swift, M.: Peeking behind the curtains of serverless platforms. In: 2018 USENIX Annual Technical Conference (USENIX ATC 2018), pp. 133–146 (2018)
25. Wang, Y., et al.: SmartHarvest: harvesting idle CPUs safely and efficiently in the cloud. In: Proceedings of the Sixteenth European Conference on Computer Systems, pp. 1–16 (2021)
26. Yu, T., et al.: Characterizing serverless platforms with serverless bench. In: Proceedings of the ACM Symposium on Cloud Computing, SoCC 2020. Association for Computing Machinery (2020). https://doi.org/10.1145/3419111.3421280

Performance Evaluation of Various RISC Processor Systems: A Case Study on ARM, MIPS and RISC-V

Yu Liu[1,2], Kejiang Ye[1(✉)], and Cheng-Zhong Xu[3]

[1] Guangdong-Hong Kong-Macao Joint Laboratory of Human-Machine
Intelligence-Synergy Systems, Shenzhen Institute of Advanced Technology,
Chinese Academy of Sciences, Shenzhen 518055, China
{liu.yu,kj.ye}@siat.ac.cn
[2] University of Chinese Academy of Sciences, Beijing 100049, China
[3] State Key Lab of IoTSC, Faculty of Science and Technology, University of Macau,
Macau SAR, China
czxu@um.edu.mo

Abstract. RISC-V is a new instruction set architecture (ISA) that has emerged in recent years. Compared with previous computer instruction architectures, RISC-V has outstanding features such as simple instructions, modular instruction set and supporting agile development. Due to these advantages, a large number of chips have been designed based on RISC-V ISA. However, compared with other ISAs, the efficiency or performance of RISC-V architecture is still not clear. In this paper, we investigate the performance difference of three mainstream RISC processor systems (i.e., ARM, MIPS and RISC-V). We use two open source benchmark tools-UnixBench and LMbench, to widely evaluate the processor performance, such as computing efficiency, read and write file delay, local communication bandwidth, etc. A total of 19 detailed performance tests on these three ISA systems are carried out. The testing results show: i) MIPS achieves the highest scores and shortest context switching delay whether it has a large number of file copying or pipeline communication; ii) RISC-V has high local communication bandwidth and strong scientific computing capabilities, but has highest communication and file access delays; iii) ARM's local communication bandwidth is low, and the delay in all aspects is slightly higher than that of MIPS.

Keywords: ISA · RISC-V · ARM · MIPS

1 Introduction

An Instruction Set Architecture (ISA) is part of the abstract model of a computer. It defines how software controls the CPU. A Reduced Instruction Set Computer (RISC), is a computer with a small, highly optimized set of instructions. The main distinguishing feature of RISC architecture is that the instruction set

© Springer Nature Switzerland AG 2022
K. Ye and L.-J. Zhang (Eds.): CLOUD 2021, LNCS 12989, pp. 61–74, 2022.
https://doi.org/10.1007/978-3-030-96326-2_5

is optimized with a large number of registers and a highly regular instruction pipeline, allowing a low number of clock cycles per instruction (CPI). There are many varieties of RISC designs include ARM [1], MIPS [2], RISC-V [3], etc.

ARM is a family of RISC architectures for computer processors, configured for various environments [1]. Arm Ltd. develops the architecture and licenses it to other companies, who design their own products that implement one of those architectures - including systems-on-chips (SoC) and systems-on-modules (SoM) that incorporate different components such as memory, interfaces, and radios. ARM processors are desirable for light, portable, battery-powered devices including smartphones, laptops and tablet computers, as well as other embedded systems, due to their low costs, minimal power consumption, and lower heat generation than their competitors.

MIPS is also a popular RISC instruction set architecture, which was developed by MIPS Computer Systems [2]. MIPS means "Microprocessor without interlocked piped stages", and its mechanism is to use software methods as much as possible to avoid data-related problems in the pipeline. In the design concept, MIPS emphasizes the collaboration of software and hardware to improve performance while simplifying hardware design.

However, the above two ISAs have also shown different weakness. For example, although the ARM instruction set is open, the authorization price is too high. At the same time, the instruction set architecture needs to be updated to forward compatibility and gradually become redundant. Therefore, in 2010, the research team at the University of California, Berkeley developed a new instruction set for the project, which is RISC-V instruction set [3].

RISC-V is an open standard ISA based on established RISC principles [4]. Unlike most other ISA designs, the RISC-V ISA is provided under open source licenses that do not require fees to use. Besides, RISC-V has other outstanding features such as simple instructions, modular instruction set and supporting agile development [5]. Due to these advantages, a large number of chip designs based on RISC-V instruction architecture have emerged. However, compared with other instruction architectures, the efficiency or performance of RISC-V instruction set architecture is still not clear. Although there are some related work on the performance evaluation on different ISAs, e.g. ARM is widely compared with the X86 ISA [6,7], there is still a lack of horizontal comparison of mainstream instruction set architecture systems.

Thus, in this paper, we investigate the performance difference of three different RISC processor systems (i.e., ARM, MIPS and RISC-V). The main contributions are summarized as follows:

- We firstly propose an evaluation methodology and build up a Docker-based unify virtualization environment for comparing the performance of three different ISA systems.
- We then use two open source benchmark tools-UnixBench and LMbench, to widely evaluate the processor performance, such as computing efficiency, read and write file delay, local communication bandwidth, etc. A total of 19 detailed performance tests are carried out.

– Key experimental findings include: i) MIPS achieves the high scores and short context switching delay whether it has a large number of file copying or pipeline communication; ii) RISC-V has high local communication bandwidth and strong scientific computing capabilities, but has high communication and file access delays; iii) ARM's local communication bandwidth is low, and the delay in all aspects is slightly higher than that of MIPS.

The rest of the paper is organized as follows. Section 2 introduces background and related work. Section 3 introduces the experimental method. Section 4 presents the experimental results. Finally, Sect. 5 concludes the whole paper and presents the future work.

2   Background and Related Work

2.1   ARM ISA

ARM instruction architecture is currently having the leading market share in the RISC instruction set family, accounting for 75% of 32-bit embedded processors. In the ARM family, some processors have not previously been able to perform floating-point arithmetic in hardware for a variety of reasons, including low power consumption and package restrictions. Today, the new generation of processors with floating point units is called the ARMhf architecture, which is used in this study.

2.2   MIPS ISA

MIPS [8] architecture was developed by Stanford University more than 20 years ago, and is widely used in many electronic products, network equipment, personal entertainment devices and commercial devices. It contains a large number of registers, instructions and characters, and the visible pipeline delay time slot. These features enable the MIPS architecture provide high performance per square millimeter and low energy consumption in today's SoC design. There are only three types of MIPS instructions, R, I and J, and the instruction format is shown in Table 1.

Table 1. Types of MIPS instructions

Type	format (32 bits)					
R	opcode(6)	rs(5)	rt(5)	rd(5)	shamt(5)	funct(6)
I	opcode(6)	rs(5)	rt(5)	immediate(16)		
J	opcode(6)	address(26)				

2.3   RISC-V ISA

RISC-V [9,10] is one of many different open architectures, but it has particular advantages, which distinguishes it from other. At first it is completely free, it uses Berkeley Software Distribution (BSD) open-source license. That makes RISC-V more attractive for the commercial use. Another important thing is the software support. RISC-V community provides a complete software stack-compiler tool chains, suitable Integrated Development Environment (IDE) and operating systems, which can be handled in embedded application. RISC-V has a widely documented hardware and software ecosystem. Base specification is now frozen, so ISA is very stable. Because of this, software written for RISC-V will run on all similar RISC-V compliant cores now and in the future.

2.4   Benchmarks

Benchmarking is a scientific methodology used to test performance indicators of different but identical types of testing subjects [11]. The testing results should have three characteristics: *Quantifiable, Repeatability, Comparability.*

There are many different types of benchmarks, in this article, we use two types of testing tools, which are *UnixBench* and *LMbench.*

UnixBench [12] is a benchmark suite that can be used to evaluate the overall performance of Unix-like systems, which is originated in 1995. In the UnixBench benchmark suite, several different tests are carried out to evaluate the performance of the system. Since it is a system benchmark, its results will not only be affected by hardware, but also operating systems, libraries, and even compilers [13]. Based on the scores of the above-mentioned different tests, a system level score (System Benchmarks Index Score) is calculated. In this study, we use this system level score to compare the performance of different systems. The testing items are shown in the Table 2.

Table 2. Items of UnixBench

UnixBench	Test items
A	Dhrystone 2 using register variables
B	Double-Precision Whetstone
C	Shell Scripts (1 concurrent)
D	Shell Scripts (8 concurrent)
E	Execl Throughput
F	File Copy 1024 bufsize 2000 maxblocks
G	File Copy 256 bufsize 500 maxblocks
H	File Copy 4096 bufsize 8000 maxblocks
I	Pipe Throughput
J	Pipe-based Context Switching
K	Process Creation
L	System Call Overhead

LMbench [14,15] a mini-measurement tool for UNIX/POSIX developed according to ANSI/C standards, contains seven different types of tests. LMbench provides a suite of benchmarks that attempt to measure the most commonly found performance bottlenecks in a wide range of system applications. These bottlenecks have been identified, isolated, and reproduced in a set of small microbenchmarks, which measure system latency and bandwidth of data movement among the processor and memory, network, file system, and disk. The intent is to produce numbers that real applications can reproduce, rather than the frequently quoted and somewhat less reproducible marketing performance numbers. The testing items are shown in Table 3.

Table 3. Items of LMbench

Benchmark	Test items
LMbench	Processor and Processes performance
	Basic integer/float/double operations performance
	Context switching performance
	Communication latencies
	File and VM system latencies
	Local communication bandwidth

2.5   QEMU

QEMU [16,17] is an open source virtual machine software that has cross-platform features and can perform hardware virtualization. It has two virtual modes: *system* mode and *user* mode. In user mode, QEMU can use the TCG (Trusted Platform Module) module of the kernel code to translated and converted heterogeneous application's Binary code. In the system mode, it can compile and run through internal modules to complete the simulation of the computer hardware system, including processor, memory, I/O devices, etc., to provide users with an abstract and virtual hardware environment. Then run the corresponding virtual machine on top of this simulation layer. In addition, its system mode is usually combined with KVM, calling the host's hardware resource KVM by sending commands to the host's interface.

In this study, to provide a unified testing environment, the system is constructed in a container, so the hardware of the host system is not directly accessed, but a virtual processor is constructed through the QEMU system model.

2.6   Related Work

There have been a number of works investigating the performance of ARM chips in server market [18,19] and on scientific computing codes [20]. Wang et al. [7]

evaluated the performance of a 64-bit ARM processor and Intel Xeon processor on Floating point computing power, memory access bandwidth and latency. The testing results shows that compared with Intel Xeon processors, ARM processors still have a lot of room for improvement in memory access latency, cache access bandwidth and latency.

There have been many works about MIPS processors performance [21,22]. Luo et al. [23] compared Loongson-3A system with Intel i5, aimed at the performance of OpenMP constructors. This research proved that Loongson 3A's performance is nearly one tenth of i5's, and results may affected by the type of compiler.

As for RISC-V, there have been studies on RISC-V chips used for acceleration of specific applications. Chen et al. [24] proposed a RISC-V processor for high-performance computing and compared with the ARM processor, Cortex-A73. In the comparison of multiple benchmarks, the results show that the performance of the RISC-V processor with instruction expansion and optimized compiler is slightly better than that of the ARM processor in the AI scenario. However, there is still lack of general proposed processor systems testings and comparison.

These studies motivate us to explore the horizontal comparison of different RISC processor systems, which is still unclear. In this paper, we tested ARM, MIPS and RISC-V processor system and compared their system performance in many aspects comprehensively, mainly includes latency, bandwidth and computing ability.

3   Experimental Methodology

In this study, the experimental environment was built through Docker image construction. Figure 1 shows the testing environment built through the above steps. The main construction steps are as follows:

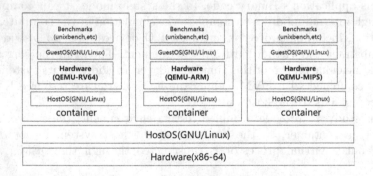

Fig. 1. Experimental environment

1. Build a Linux system in the Docker images and load QEMU. LXC (Linux Container) is a kind of kernel virtualization technology that realizes the resource virtualization at the Linux operating system level. Docker encapsulates the underlying technology of LXC, implements resource isolation through namespaces, and implements resource restrictions through cgroups.
2. Use QEMU to build virtual hardware, set parameters, and determine the configuration of the virtual system. Virtual hardware mainly includes processor, memory and I/O. Different instruction set architectures are set through the built-in processor emulator of QEMU, and the conversion of processor instructions is realized through dynamic converters inside, so as to adapt to different host processors. At the same time, MMU of the target system is simulated internally by using the mmap() system interface; while the QEMU simulation hardware is initialized, the PIO space is registered through the register_ioport_read(), register_ioport_write() functions, and the EPT mechanism of the virtual machine is used to Register in the MMIO space.
3. After the virtual system is built, download and run two sets of testing suites: UnixBench [12] and LMbench [14]. UnixBench items are shown in Table 2. The running mechanism of applications in Docker containers is different from that in hosts. Multiple containers may run many applications, sharing resources of one or more underlying hosts. Therefore we run three containers in the same environment, but run the benchmark at different times to avoid resource contention between them, which may affect the testing performance.
4. Get running testing results, compare and analyze the testing results.

4 Experimental Results

4.1 UnixBench

Firstly, we tested the operating performance of single-core with different processor architectures, and compared their differences. Then we tested the system performance when running all the processor cores of the system. A total of 12 sub-items were tested in Table 2, and the Y-axis of the graph represents system benchmarks score.

It can be seen from Fig. 2 that for a single-core testing, RISC-V's string processing and floating-point calculation capabilities (i.e., A and B) are significantly better than ARM and MIPS, especially the string processing capability score, which is almost double of scores of ARM. At the same time, RISC-V is nearly two times higher than the previous two in terms of floating-point computing performance testing scores. This reflects the computing power of RISC-V processor system. In the shell script testing, RISC-V is slightly better than MIPS, and MIPS is slightly better than ARM system whether it is to operate 1 or 8 scripts (i.e., C, D) at the same time. However, in the testing of file copy transmission (i.e., F, G, and H), MIPS scored the highest, followed by ARM, and RISC-V's performance was far inferior to the previous two. Whether it was using 256M 1024M or 4096M buffer, it seems that RISC-V performs poorly in terms of memory. In the Pipeline Throughput Test (i.e., I), the testing measures the number of times a process writes 512 bits into the pipe per second and reads back per second. ARM and MIPS perform equally well, and RISC-V scores in this category. It is much lower. For the process creation test and the pipeline-based context switching test (i.e., J and K), RISC-V scored the highest, followed by MIPS, and ARM scored the lowest. In the system call consumption test, (i.e., L) MIPS scored the highest, followed by ARM, and finally RISC-V.

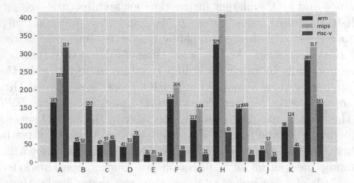

Fig. 2. Single core comparison

Figure 3 mainly shows the comparison results of complete systems used three ISAs. It can be seen from that scores of RISC-V processor systems had significant improvement. In Fig. 3, it can be seen that in the performance of string processing and floating-point computing capabilities, RISC-V has further expanded the advantages of ARM and MIPS. The score of RISC-V string processing is nearly four times that of ARM, three times that of MIPS. And the score of floating-point operations is nearly six times that of ARM and MIPS. In the shell script tests, the performance of RISC-V only increased slightly, but it performed better than the other two systems. In the Excel throughput test, the scores of the three systems are similar, but RISC-V is even slightly better. However, for file transfer tests that use a large number of caches, MIPS still performs best, followed by ARM, slightly lower than MIPS, and RISC-V the lowest. The score of MIPS in the 256M buffer is more than three times that of RISC-V, 1024M is nearly four times that of RISC-V, and 4096M is more than twice that of RISC-V. In the subsequent tests, RISC-V scores have improved to varying degrees, but the overall score is still lower than the first two. In the last system call consumption test, MIPS scored the highest, RISC-V followed, and ARM scored the lowest.

Through the above testings, we can find that RISC-V is better than MIPS and ARM in processor performance; but in terms of system interface calls and file transfer, MIPS is slightly better than ARM and much better than RISC-V. It can be seen that when the number of processor cores of RISC-V doubles, the scores of various testings are almost doubled, and the performance is improved by nearly 100%, except for the shell script test, which only increased by about 13%.

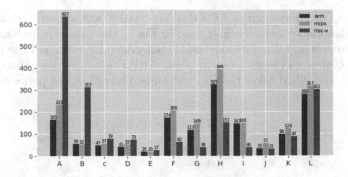

Fig. 3. Complete system comparison

4.2 LMbench

The testing suite mainly includes bandwidth testing tools and delay testing tools, totally including 7 experiments. The testing results is the average value after three tests.

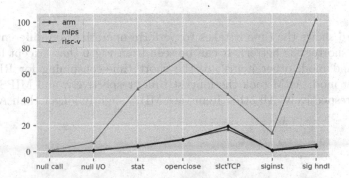

Fig. 4. File related processing performance (ms)

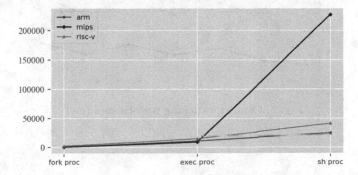

Fig. 5. Process operation performance (ms)

In Fig. 4, the performance of ARM and MIPS are almost the same, and RISC-V takes longer than the first two; in Fig. 5, the time-consuming to create the same process and simulate the shell is not much different, and the process of asking the system to create a new process, MIPS takes the most time, followed by RISC-V, and ARM takes the shortest time. Overall, ARM performs best.

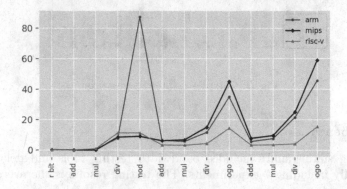

Fig. 6. Basic integer/float/double operations performance (ns)

Figure 6 shows the time it takes to perform operations on different types of data (the shorter the better). It can be seen from Fig. 6 that, except for integer division and mod, other items are the short time-consuming for RISC-V. In the integer mod, ARM took the longest time, respectively, and MIPS took the shortest, respectively. All other items are MIPS slightly longer than ARM.

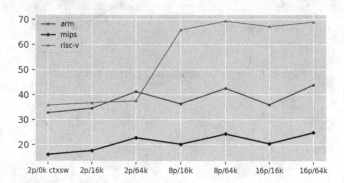

Fig. 7. Context switching performance (ms)

The testing result in Fig. 7 shows that MIPS has the best context switching performance. In the case of different sizes and number of processes, the time-consuming gap between MIPS and ARM is exactly the same. However, RISC-V takes slightly less time than ARM in the case of two processes, each of which is 64k, and other items are take the longest.

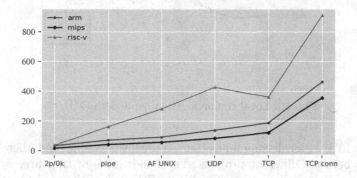

Fig. 8. Communication latencies (ms)

It can be seen from Fig. 8 that different protocols are used for inter-process communication. MIPS still takes the shortest time, followed by ARM and RISC-V takes longest time.

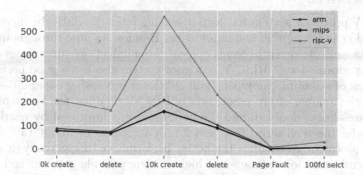

Fig. 9. File and VM latencies (ms)

It can be seen from Fig. 9 that overall, RISC-V has the longest time delay for file generation and memory, followed by ARM, and MIPS has the shortest time delay. There is a big gap between the time-consuming ARM and MIPS to create 10k files.

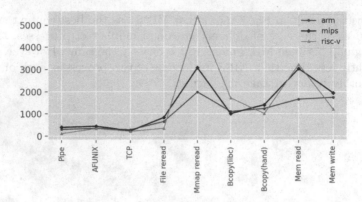

Fig. 10. Local communication bandwidth (MB/s)

Figure 10 is a local communication bandwidth testing, and there is a big difference between different projects. The bandwidths of the three systems in the first three items are similar. The bandwidth rank of the read file is MIPS > ARM > RISC-V, and the bandwidth rank of the mapped file is RISC-V > MIPS > ARM. The rank of memory copy performance is RISC-V > ARM > MIPS, the rank of disk copy performance is MIPS > ARM > RISC-V. All in all, in the communication bandwidth testing, because each item involves different parts of the system such as memory and disk, the performance is very different.

4.3   Discussion

- RISC-V processor system has high operating latency, relatively, including file operation and computer communication. Besides, its pipe throughout tests is also not well. However, in terms of local communication, some types of bandwidth performed well, RISC-V processor system also has a good performance in terms of scientific computing and character processing capabilities.
- When the number of processor cores of RISC-V doubles, the scores of various tests are almost doubled, and the performance is improved by nearly 100%, except for the shell script test, which only increased by about 13%.
- MIPS processor system has the better performance, respectively, it achieved high scores and low latency and high efficiency in file copying and pipeline throughput.
- Performance of ARM processor system is similar to which of MIPS except handful items, and a little worse than that of MIPS processor system. They both have low operating latency and low character processing capabilities, relatively.

5   Conclusion and Future Work

In this paper, we first analyzed the current popular instruction set architectures (i.e., ARM, MIPS and RISC-V) in detail. Then two testing units were used to test these different architectures in detail. We built an unify testing environment based on Docker images, installed testing tools in the operating system, and started monitoring objects according to the information specified in the configuration to monitor the resource consumption of system running programs. By comparing system performance scores in different testing cases, corresponding conclusions can be obtained. Based on the analysis results, some possible performance optimization schemes were given.

RISC-V performed very well in the computing power of the processor, and part of the local communication bandwidth also performs well, but the time delay is not as good as the other two ISAs. The performance of MIPS and ARM in each test is relatively similar, their latency is low, and file operation is well, but in general, MIPS is slightly better.

In the future, different processor systems can be improved for poor performance according to the testing performance. For example, MIPS can further improve numerical computing capabilities, ARM can better adapt to specific communication protocols, thereby increasing communication bandwidth, and RISC-V can increase instruction read speed, thereby reducing system operation latency.

Acknowledgment. This work is supported by Key-Area Research and Development Program of Guangdong Province (NO. 2020B010164003), National Natural Science Foundation of China (No. 62072451), Shenzhen Basic Research Program (No. JCYJ20200109115418592), Science and Technology Development Fund of Macao S.A.R (FDCT) under number 0015/2019/AKP, and Youth Innovation Promotion Association CAS (NO. 2019349).

References

1. Seal, D.: ARM Architecture Reference Manual. Pearson Education, London (2001)
2. Hennessy, J., et al.: MIPS: a microprocessor architecture. ACM SIGMICRO Newslett. **13**(4), 17–22 (1982)
3. Asanović, K., Patterson, D.A.: Instruction sets should be free: the case for RISC-V. EECS Department, University of California, Berkeley, Technical Report. UCB/EECS-2014-146, 2014
4. Greengard, S.: Will RISC-V revolutionize computing? Commun. ACM **63**(5), 30–32 (2020)
5. Lee, Y., et al.: An agile approach to building RISC-V microprocessors. IEEE Micro **36**(2), 8–20 (2016)
6. Aroca, R.V., Gonçalves, L.M.G.: Towards green data centers: a comparison of ×86 and arm architectures power efficiency. J. Parallel Distrib. Comput. **72**(12), 1770–1780 (2012)
7. Wang, Y., Liao, Q., Zuo, S., Xie, R., Lin, X.: Performance evaluation of ARM-ISA SoC for high performance computing. Comput. Sci. **46**(8), 95–99 (2019)
8. Ma, H., Wang, D.: The design of five-stage pipeline CPU based on MIPS. In: 2011 International Conference on Electrical and Control Engineering, pp. 433–435. IEEE (2011)

9. Asanovic, K., Waterman, A.: The RISC-V instruction set manual. In: Privileged Architecture, Document Version 20190608-Priv-MSU-Ratified, volume 2. RISC-V Foundation (2019)
10. Patsidis, K., Konstantinou, D., Nicopoulos, C., Dimitrakopoulos, G.: A low-cost synthesizable RISC-V dual-issue processor core leveraging the compressed instruction set extension. Microprocess. Microsyst. **61**, 1–10 (2018)
11. Jiang, Z.: A linux server operating system's performance comparison using LMbench. In: 2016 International Conference on Network and Information Systems for Computers (ICNISC), pp. 160–164. IEEE (2016)
12. Duplyakin, D., Uta, A., Maricq, A., Ricci, R.: On studying CPU performance of CloudLab hardware. In: 27th IEEE International Conference on Network Protocols. ICNP 2019, Chicago, IL, USA, 8–10 October 2019, pp. 1–2. IEEE (2019)
13. Lucas, K.: UnixBench, 30 August 2016. https://github.com/kdlucas/byteunixbench
14. McVoy, L.W., Staelin, C., et al.: LMbench: portable tools for performance analysis. In: USENIX Annual Technical Conference, pp. 279–294, San Diego (1996)
15. Staelin, C.: LMbench: an extensible micro-benchmark suite. Softw. Pract. Experience **35**(11), 1079–1105 (2005)
16. Bellard, F.: QEMU, a fast and portable dynamic translator. In: USENIX Annual Technical Conference, FREENIX Track, vol. 41, p. 46, California (2005)
17. No, J., Park, S.: Multi-layered I/O virtualization cache on KVM/QEMU. In: 2019 Eleventh International Conference on Ubiquitous and Future Networks (ICUFN), pp. 695–699. IEEE (2019)
18. Coppola, M., Falsafi, B., Goodacre, J., Kornaros, G.: From embedded multi-core SoCs to scale-out processors. In: 2013 Design, Automation Test in Europe Conference Exhibition (DATE), pp. 947–951 (2013)
19. Stanley-Marbell, P., Cabezas, V.C.: Performance, power, and thermal analysis of low-power processors for scale-out systems. In: 25th IEEE International Symposium on Parallel and Distributed Processing. IPDPS 2011, Anchorage, Alaska, USA, 16–20 May 2011 - Workshop Proceedings, pp. 863–870. IEEE (2011)
20. Abdurachmanov, D., Bockelman, B., Elmer, P., Eulisse, G., Knight, R., Muzaffar, S.: Heterogeneous high throughput scientific computing with APM X-Gene and intel Xeon Phi. CoRR abs/1410.3441 (2014)
21. Songhori, E.M., Zeitouni, S., Dessouky, G., Schneider, T., Sadeghi, A.-R., Koushanfar, F.: GarbledCPU: a MIPS processor for secure computation in hardware. In: Proceedings of the 53rd Annual Design Automation Conference. DAC 2016, Austin, TX, USA, 5–9 June 2016, pp. 73:1–73:6. ACM (2016)
22. Takamaeda-Yamazaki, S., Nakatsuka, H., Tanaka, Y., Kise, K.: Ultrasmall: a tiny soft processor architecture with multi-bit serial datapaths for FPGAs. IEICE Trans. Inf. Syst. **98-D**(12), 2150–2158 (2015)
23. Luo, Q., Kong, C., Cai, Y., Liu, G.: Performance evaluation of OpenMP constructs and kernel benchmarks on a Loongson-3A Quad-Core SMP system. In: 2011 12th International Conference on Parallel and Distributed Computing, Applications and Technologies, pp. 191–196 (2011)
24. Chen, C., et al.: Xuantie-910: a commercial multi-core 12-stage pipeline out-of-order 64-bit high performance RISC-V processor with vector extension: industrial product. In: 47th ACM/IEEE Annual International Symposium on Computer Architecture. ISCA 2020, Valencia, Spain, 30 May–3 June 3 2020, pp. 52–64. IEEE (2020)

Comparative Analysis of Cloud Storage Options for Diverse Application Requirements

Antara Debnath Antu[1], Anup Kumar[1(⊠)], Robert Kelley[2], and Bin Xie[3]

[1] Department of Computer Science and Engineering,
University of Louisville, Louisville, KY, USA
ak@louisville.edu
[2] Department of Computer Science, Bellarmine University, Louisville, KY, USA
[3] InfoBeyond Technology LLC, Louisville, KY, USA

Abstract. Cloud Storage is the concept of combining and sharing of storage resources through the Internet. Each cloud service provider (CSP) offers universal data storage services using its geographically distributed datacenters. Businesses and consumers are increasingly reliant on cloud-based storage solutions instead of in-house, on-premises local storage hardware in order to save on initial expenditures to build and maintain the hardware infrastructures. Cloud Storage provides enormous levels of data protection and important data can be restored in case of missing local copies. Selecting the right public cloud provider has become critical to long term business success. Depending on the different business needs and requirements of these storage services, we compare a few of the storage services provided by three market giants like Amazon Web Services, Microsoft Windows Azure and Google Cloud Platform.

Keywords: Cloud Storage · Amazon Web Services · Microsoft Azure · Google Cloud Platform · Flexible storage solutions

1 Introduction

In the last decade, businesses have been moving away from local systems for storing and processing data to cloud-based systems due to the massive increase in the amount of data the typical business needs to operate. Designing, implementing, and maintaining data storage systems is a complicated endeavor. To mitigate these risks, companies are replacing their local data centers with cloud storage which offers innumerable ways to store, serve, and process data. And a significant benefit is that cloud storage providers (CSPs) typically offer data storage at low cost or no cost.

Cloud storage is assisted by cloud computing, e.g., running workloads within a cloud environment over the Internet. The primary advantage of access to cloud storage doesn't require an intranet connection or a direct connection to storage hardware [1]. Instead, connections to the data are made over the existing infrastructure of the Internet.

Cloud storage is popular in every sector of industry and has several advantages including: unlimited storage, updated operating systems, affordability, and ease of access to the data from anywhere in the world. Data can be easily retrieved in case of serious technology failure or a victim of a catastrophic human error. Not only do large companies benefit from cloud storage, but startups are taking advantage of cloud services that provide pay-as-you-go pricing plans and instant scaling up or down of computing resources as required.

Unfortunately, the existing cloud services market is vast, with myriad providers that offer an overwhelming number of services. To reduce the difficulty of selecting the right provider for various scenarios, we analyze the offerings of the most used providers in cloud computing which includes Amazon Web Services (AWS) [3], Microsoft Azure [4] and Google Cloud Platform (GCP) [5]. Of the three, AWS is currently the leading cloud provider. However, both Azure and Google cloud use are rapidly increasing [2]. Table 1 gives a glimpse of comparative evaluation of data storage options provided by AWS, Microsoft Azure and Google Cloud.

The primary contribution of this paper is that we present direct comparison of the products and services of the "Big Three" providers to assist practitioners with choosing the correct provider/service for various scenarios. Each section of this paper consists of a broad description of a class of storage with similar resources and characteristics and gives a cumulative assessment of the services each provider delivers in that category.

The remainder of this paper is outlined as follows: Sect. 2 introduces various types of Object Storage, Sect. 3 presents Block Storage services, and Sect. 4 presents various Message Storage services. Section 5 introduces various Relational Database services and Sect. 6 introduces NoSQL Data Storage services. Section 7 presents Manage Data Warehouse services. Finally, Sect. 8 concludes our paper.

Table 1. Different storage options provided by the AWS, Microsoft Azure and Google cloud.

Storage Type	Vendors		
	AWS	Azure	Google Platform
Object Storage	Amazon Simple Storage Service (S3) ⊃ S3 Standard ⊃ S3 Intelligent-Tiering ⊃ S3 Standard-IA ⊃ S3 One Zone-IA ⊃ S3 Glacier ⊃ S3 Glacier Deep Archive	Azure Blob Storage ⊃ Block blobs ⊃ Append blobs ⊃ Page blobs	Google Cloud Storage ⊃ Standard Storage ⊃ Nearline Storage ⊃ Coldline Storage ⊃ Archive Storage
Block Storage	Elastic Block Store (EBS)	Azure managed Disk	Cloud Persistent Disk
Message Service	Simple Queue Service	Azure Queue Storage	Google Cloud Pub/sub
Relational Database	Amazon RDS ⊃ Amazon Aurora	Azure SQL Database	Cloud SQL
No SQL Database	DynamoDB/SimpleDB	Azure Table Storage	⊃ Cloud Datastore ⊃ Cloud Big Table
Managed Data Warehouse	Redshift	Azure Synapse	Big Query

2 Object Storage

Object storage is a type of data storage architecture for processing data as objects and for storing unstructured data in the cloud. In object storage, the data is divided into separate units called objects and is reserved in a single source. Each object generally contains the data, a changeable number of metadata and a universally unique identifier. That means, objects can be stored across numerous storage devices and various locations and can be requested from any place through its identifier even if it is not in the same physical location from where the request was sent before. Cloud-based object storage services typically offer simple, pre-defined tiers with diverse levels of storage capacity and workload performance (Input/output operations per second, or IOPS) as it is elastic, flexible and offers multiple availability zones. Data protection and duplication to other data centers for business endurance is possible with an expected monthly fee. Anyone can increase or decrease IOPS and expand data volumes dynamically [6].

2.1 Amazon Simple Storage Service (S3)

Amazon S3 is a storage service that offers the highest level of data scalability, availability, durability, security, and top-notch performance at the customer end. It is designed for 99.999% of durability and stored data is automatically distributed across a minimum of three physical services that are geologically separated by a minimum of 10 km within an AWS Region, and can automatically replicate data to another AWS Region [9]. S3 provides security standards and compliance certifications to satisfy compliance obligations. The S3 Inventory tool distributes organized reports and can analyze object access patterns to build lifecycle policies that automate tiering, deletion, and retaining. Amazon S3 works with AWS Lambda, without dealing with any additional set-up. Customers can run significant analytics of data without extracting or moving into a separate analytics database [8]. Developers also can easily use this service as it makes web-scale computing easier. Amazon S3 offers a series of storage based on different uses and for different types of data. Pricing depends on in terms of hot, warm, or cold data. Less frequently accessed data are cold data, and it is cheaper to store than the data which is frequently accessed on a daily basis or hot data. Companies can easily move data between these storage options anytime to optimize their storage costs. Several Amazon S3 choices [10] are the following:

Amazon S3 Standard: The best storage option for data frequently accessed and general-purpose uses as it provides low latency and high throughput. S3 Storage class has developed at the object level through which a single bucket can stores objects across S3 Standard, S3 Intelligent-Tiering, S3 Standard-IA, and S3 One Zone-IA. Enterprises also use S3 Lifecycle policies because without any application changing or data interruption, objects transition between storage classes are automatic.

Amazon S3 Intelligent-Tiering: The S3 Intelligent-Tiering stores object into two access tiers. One of them is designed for frequent access and another tier is cost-effective and designed for less frequent access. With a small monthly charge, Amazon S3 monitors available patterns of the objects in S3 Intelligent-Tiering and transfers data that have not been accessed for 30 sequential days to the infrequent access tier. When an object is accessed further, it automatically transferred back to the frequent access tier. No data recovery charges, and additional tiering fees are necessary when using the S3 Intelligent-Tiering storage class or when objects are relocated between access tiers. It is the ultimate storage class for long-lived data with advanced design patterns that are unfamiliar or random.

Amazon S3 Standard-Infrequent Access: S3 Standard-IA is designed for data that is not needed very often but requires frequent access when needed. S3 Standard-IA offers very minimum fees per GB storage and data retrieval with vast durability and high throughput. These facilities make S3 Standard-IA supreme for long-term storage, data backups, and disaster recovery.

Amazon S3 One Zone-Infrequent Access: S3 One Zone-IA is nearly the same as S3 Standard-IA, but the only difference is it stores data in three Availability Zones (AZs). When it stores data only one AZ, the price is 20% less than S3 Standard-IA. Customers who want a low-cost option for occasionally used data but do not have the priority of data availability and elasticity, S3 One Zone-IA is beneficial for them.

Amazon S3 Glacier: S3 Glacier is a secure storage class for data archiving. It is designed for long-term storage of rarely accessed data. To maintain minimum price yet fit for various needs, S3 Glacier provides three data retrieval choices that differ from a few minutes to hours. Customers can directly upload the objects to S3 Glacier or can use the S3 Lifecycle plan to move data to any of the S3 Storage Classes for active data.

Amazon S3 Glacier Deep Archive: S3 Glacier Deep Archive is the lowest-cost storage and supports long-term data holding and protection that may be accessed once or twice in a year. This storage selection is right for customers who save data for 7–10 years or longer for regulatory compliance requirements. All objects are replicated and stored across at least three globally distributed AZs and can be restored within 12 h.

2.2 Azure Blob Storage

Azure Blob storage is Microsoft's scalable object-based storage solution for the cloud. Blobs are low-level data primitives that are optimized for storing and serving massive amounts of unstructured data. Blob storage is perfect for executing images or documents directly to a browser and stored data can be analyzed by an onsite or Azure-hosted service. Customers can retrieve objects via HTTP/HTTPS at any time throughout the world. An Azure account is required to get the storage access and can work both as a general-purpose storage account or a blob account. The storage account is distributed into containers, which are equivalent of folders in regular MS Windows OS and the files stored in containers are called "blobs". Blobs are of 3 different types: block, append, and page [12]. Users must specify the blob type when creates the blob. Once the blob has been created, its type cannot be changed, and it can be modified only by using suitable operations for that blob type. Blob replaces the changes immediately. Each version of the blob has an exclusive tag (ETag), that gives assurance that users can only change a specific instance of the blob with certain conditions. Any blob can be leased for exclusive write access and duplicated in a snapshot. Objects in Blob storage are reachable via the Azure Storage REST API, Azure CLI, Azure PowerShell or an Azure Storage client library [11].

Block Blobs: Block blobs store blocks of data, specifically text, and binary data. It contained blocks and can be identified by a block ID. Customers can create or modify a block blob by writing a set of blocks and combining them with their block IDs. Each block can be a different size and a block blob can include up to 50,000 blocks and up to 4.7 TB of data. It helps users to manage large files over networks and upload numerous blocks in parallel in any order to get minimum upload time and control their sequence in the final block list step. When a block blob upload is larger than the value in this space, storage clients split the file into blocks. Users can add a new block and replace an existing uncommitted block of the same block ID. New blocks remain in an unchanged state until they are precisely stored or discarded.

Append Blobs: It includes blocks like block blobs but is specifically for append services. Blocks are smaller than block blobs but optimized for several I/O operations. Append blobs are ideal for circumstances like logging data from virtual machines. Using append blob operation, when it is needed to modify, blocks are added to the end of the blob only. Changing or deleting current blocks is not supported. Unlike a block blob, an append blob does not reveal its block IDs.

Page Blobs: Page blobs include 512-byte pages which are necessary for random read/write storage and can be up to 8 TB in size 12. To create a page blob, customers adjust the page blob and declare the highest size of the page blob. Except for a few minor changes, the API for the page blobs is the same as the block blob. It stores virtual hard drive (VHD) files and Azure virtual machine disks are backed by page blobs. Azure manages two types of durable disk storage: premium and standard. Premium storage is developed for Azure virtual machine workloads that need consistent high performance and low latency.

2.3 Google Cloud Storage

Google Cloud is an application integrated and object-oriented storage for developers and organizations. It is focused on conventional Internet applications and splits the computational and storage components through the application. Google Cloud inspires developers to create applications precisely for the cloud using commercial technologies. It provides optimize price and performance across storage classes where projects are used to store all data and buckets are the data containers that store objects [13]. For best performance, Google provides worldwide storage classes, which are appropriate for frequently used objects and reachable from any locations. Since Google cloud uses region-specific buckets, developers have higher regulatory access to the performance of data operations. Google only creates restrictions on the rate of bucket operations for a project, but not the number of buckets that have created for a single project. Within every 2 s, only 1 operation can be done with a bucket, so developers are encouraged to work with objects instead of buckets. Google cloud offers different storage classes like Standard, Nearline, Coldline, Archive which are based on different object's availability and pricing model.

Standard Storage: Standard Storage is the best option for frequently accessed data or hot data and stored for only short periods for general use. It is the right choice for storing data in the same location as Google Kubernetes Engine (GKE) can use the data. GKE provides an organized environment using Google frame to form a cluster. In the multi-region scenario, Standard Storage is also suitable for storing data that is accessible worldwide.

Nearline Storage: Nearline Storage is a low-cost, highly robust storage service for storing the data which is not used frequently or cold data. It offers moderate accessibility, 30-day minimum storage duration. Data that are not used on a regular basis and need to be read or modified on average once per month or less, nearline storage is perfect for them. It is also suitable for data backup and archiving.

Coldline Storage: Coldline Storage is very economical, and it offers a 90-day minimum storage duration, slightly lower accessibility than standard storage. It is ideal for data that need to use or change at most once a quarter and focuses only on data backup or archiving purposes.

Archive Storage: Archive Storage is the lowest cost for data archiving, online data backup, and disaster recovery. It has no availability SLA like other cloud storage classes and data accessibility is like Nearline Storage and Coldline Storage. Archive Storage offers a 365-day minimum storage duration. It is the best choice for data which will be necessary to access less than once a year. In Table 2, a detailed comparison of Object Storage options which are Amazon S3, Azure Blob and Google Cloud Storage have presented.

Table 2. Comparison of several object storage.

Features	Object storage		
	Amazon S3	Azure blob	Google cloud
Hot	S3 standard	Hot blob storage	Standard cloud storage
Cool	S3 standard-infrequent access	Cool blob storage	Nearline cloud storage
Archive	Amazon Glacier	Archive blob storage	Archive cloud storage
Storage size	5 TB/Object	4.77 TB/Object	5 TB/Object
Regions	22 locations	56 locations	20 locations

(*continued*)

Table 2. (*continued*)

Features	Object storage		
	Amazon S3	Azure blob	Google cloud
Access API	S3 API	S3-compatible (using s3proxy)	S3-compatible
Latency	Milliseconds	Milliseconds	Milliseconds
Object limit	Unlimited	Unlimited	Unlimited
Availability	99.999%	99.95%	99.9%
Multi-part upload	Multipart upload API	REST API tracks blob	JSON API
Object-level tagging	Available	Available	Not available
Data replication	Cross region replication	LRS, GRS and RA-GRS	Regional or multi-regional
Users purchase term	1 year/3 year	1 year/3 year	1 year/3 year: committed use

3 Block Storage

Block storage devices offer raw storage capacity with fixed-sized. Generally, block storage employed in host databases because it supports random read/write operations and keeps system files of the running virtual machines. Information is stored in volumes and blocks wherever files are divided equally into sized blocks which are distributed among the storage nodes. This similarly supports the volume I/O performance. Every block has its address, however in contrast to objects, they do not have metadata. Storage volumes are handled by external server operating systems and imagined as a separate disk drive. This block device can be mounted by the guest operating system and works like a physical disk. Public cloud suppliers permit making numerous file systems on their block storage systems to empower their users to store persistent data like a database [7].

3.1 AWS Elastic Block Store (EBS)

Amazon EBS is a storage service provider that is very popular to the user ends, easy to use and offering high-performance. It developed to use with Amazon Elastic Compute Cloud (EC2) for both throughput and transaction-concentrated jobs at any size. Wide-Ranging workloads and media workflows are largely deployed on Amazon EBS. Also, customers can achieve very minimum latency with high-performance database workloads such as SAP HANA or gigabytes/second throughput such as Hadoop [14]. EBS sizes are replicated within an Availability Zone (AZ) and can easily scale to petabytes of data. Applications such as SAP, Oracle, and Microsoft products can perform with very demanding workloads. SSD-backed volumes offer a durable price/performance for most workloads. HDD-backed volumes are designed for big data to analyze engines and managing data warehousing. By using Fast Snapshot Restore (FSR), customers can receive promptly full performance when making an EBS volume from a snapshot. EBS

Snapshots permit volumes backup and recovery for geographic safety. Data Lifecycle Manager (DLM) is an easy-to-use tool for automating snapshot management without any extra cost.

3.2 Azure Managed Disk

Azure managed disks are block-level storage that is supported by Azure and connected with Azure Virtual Machines (VMs). Managed disks are like a physical disk in an on-site server but virtualized. With this method users do not have to consider and provision the storage account limits, they will only specify the disk size, the disk type and monitor the disk. The offered categories of disks are ultra-disks, premium solid-state drives (SSD), standard SSDs, and typical hard disk drives (HDD). When users are done with their disk provisioned, the rest of the work will Azure handles and makes life easier for them. The user will not see the storage accounts any longer, they can only see the disks which connected to the VMs. Companies can use Role-based access control (RBAC), locks and tags with managed disks to be more flexible assigning the exact authorizations and providing the correct labels in their employees. Managed disks with VMs running are capable to do snapshots of current VMs. Azure Managed Disk provides a benefit when working with images as users do not need to copy the image to each storage account. They will use a new VM with managed disks from a controlled image that is stored in the central image achieve.

Table 3. Comparison of Amazon EBS, Azure managed disk, and Google persistent disk.

Features	Block storage		
	Amazon EBS	Azure managed disk	Google persistent disk
Volume types	General purpose and IOPS SSD	Ultra-disk, premium SSD, standard SSD & HDD	Zonal HDD, regional, zonal SSD, regional SSD persistent disks
Volume sizes	1 GB to 16 TiB	1 GB to 32 TiB	Up to 64 TB
Max IOPs per volume	64,000	20,000	30,000
Availability	99.99%	99.9%	99.95%
Max throughput per volume	1,000 MB/S	900 MB/S	1,200 MB/S
Data redundancy	RAID-1 (With AZs)	Locally redundant, (LRS)	Build-in redundancy
Snapshot redundancy	Multiple AZs in the region	Multiple zones in the region	Multiple locations
Snapshot locality	Regional	Global	Global
Encryption	AES-256 algorithm	AES-256 algorithm	AES-256 algorithm

3.3 Google Cloud Persistent Disk

Google Persistent Disk is a durable and high-performance block storage, and it is used by all virtual machines in Google Cloud Platform. The behavior of the Persistent Disks is like an ordinary USB drive. They can be either be Hard Disk Drive (HDD) or Solid-State Drive (SSD) with high I/O performance. HDD presents cost-effective storage and SSD offers reliably with bulk throughput. Both categories can be up to 64 TB in size. A persistent disk is imagined as the default root disk of the virtual machine and has the authority to choose where they are located and based on the different situations different accessibility is required like Regional, Zonal, or Local. This concept differs greatly from a virtual machine in the workstation, but it is relatively similar to an on-sites storage area network (SAN) storage system. It is compulsory to mention the users that these local disks are only available in the hardware where the virtual machine is running, and they are not often recommended due to the low availability. Conversely, if users require high accessibility, Regional disks will offer that immediately by replicating the disks in different zones within a region. A more moderate and cost-effective approach are Zonal disks, which are highly available but only within a single zone. Persistent Disks offers snapshot capability which can be used for both backup and virtual machine image-making. Snapshots of block disks generate in minutes in place of hours. In addition, these Persistent Disks are also used to power the GKE service and support simultaneous readers at the same time [17]. In the following Table 3, a comparison of several options of Block Storage provided by AWS, Azure and Google Cloud have displayed.

4 Message Storage

Message storage provides communication and coordination for several distributed applications. It is asynchronous and peer-to-peer communication by not involving any server service. This type of storage provides a lightweight buffer that temporarily stores messages until processed and the software connects to the queue for sending and receiving messages. The messages are usually small, such as requests, replies, error messages or just plain information. With an individual user, every message is exchanged one time only and hence this messaging pattern is usually called one-to-one, or point-to-point communications. Message queues can significantly simplify the coding of decoupled applications while improving performance [13].

4.1 Amazon Simple Queue Service (SQS)

Amazon SQS is asynchronous and synchronous messaging service which is designed for a cloud computing environment and achieves a similar goal. It sends messages using queries via the Internet which means the messages can run and collapse discretely in the path. But SQS will settle arising common issues like producer-consumer problem or connectivity between producer and consumer. A standard setup is not needed but companies must use a key management system and make logs that can be replicated in the event of a complaint. The messages use 256-bit AES (Advanced Encryption Standard) encryption to confirm the safe arrival of the messages and encryption keys are handled effectively to log encryption keys correctly [15]. For a minimum amount of message queues, SQS provides free tier. But when clients scale up, they only pay for the infrastructure needed to use. Standard and SQS FIFO are two different message queues provided by SQS. Standard supports the highest throughput, optimum collection effort, and at-least-once delivery. SQS FIFO queues are developed to assure that messages are sent with exact order [15].

4.2 Azure Queue Storage

Azure Queue is a system which is storing large numbers of messages and can be accessed worldwide by using HTTP or HTTPS [16]. A queue can contain loads of messages up to the entire maximum volume of a storage account. Queues can be used to offload background and non- communicating jobs that ultimately helps with scaling applications and in controlling sudden traffic bursts. If something went wrong in the infrastructure, then messages are buffered and automatically picked up by other message processing nodes that control the integrity of the workload. Applications delay unexpected traffic bursts, which stops servers from being overwhelmed by the overflow. The monitor queue adds flexibility to the application and arranges added worker nodes based on user demand.

4.3 Google Cloud Pub/Sub

Cloud Pub/Sub has created the capability and fidelity of enterprise-oriented message middleware to the cloud. The route for sending a message can be one-to-many (fan-out), many-to-one (fan-in), and many-to-many. By providing a many-to-many asynchronous messaging service that separates senders and receivers and permits a secure and vastly offered communication among autonomous written applications. Google Compute Engine instance can distribute a bulky message queue among multiple workers and can write logs to a database for later querying. Multi-region settings run smoothly because of Cloud Pub/Sub's global nature. An inhabited sensor can stream data to back-end servers hosted in the cloud. Pub/Sub distributes minimum latency, robust messaging that supports developers to fast integration systems which accommodated on the Google Cloud Platform and outwardly [24]. Table 4 has provided a broad comparison of Message Storage options like: Amazon SQS, Azure Queue Storage and Google Cloud Pub/Sub.

Table 4. Comparison of Amazon SQS, Azure queue storage and Google Cloud Pub/Sub.

Features	Message storage		
	Amazon SQS	Azure queue storage	Google cloud Pub/Sub
Service	Asynchronous and synchronous messaging	Asynchronous messaging	Asynchronous and synchronous messaging
Create/delete queue	Yes	Yes	Yes
Max message size	256 KB	64 KB	10 MB

(continued)

Table 4. (*continued*)

Features	Message storage		
	Amazon SQS	Azure queue storage	Google cloud Pub/Sub
Batch message	Yes	No	Yes
Update message	Yes	Yes	No
Access control	Enabled	Enabled	Enabled
Security protocol	HTTP over SSL (HTTPS) and Transport Layer Security (TLS) protocols	Using HTTP or HTTPS	HTTPS server with SSL and HTTP POST
Message retention	14 days	7 days	7 days
FIFO	Yes	Yes	No

5   Relational Database

A relational database (RDB) is a popular type of database which programmed in SQL and whose data is stored in tables. Tables are linked or related based on common data items or pre-defined relationships between them and divided into rows or records and columns or fields. A cloud-based relational database serves the same functions as a traditional relational database with updated software infrastructure and additional flexibility of cloud computing. As RDB storage offers secured, resizable capacity and cost-effective way to store the data, organizations are more willing to move their data to take benefit of several data. Automation of time-consuming tasks can be done in minutes with fast performance and high accessibility so that entrepreneurs can give utter focus on their application and business future [18].

5.1   Amazon RDS Storage

Amazon RDS is a web-based distributed relational database service offered by AWS to install, operate and maintain a relational database for use in different applications. It also can integrate with Amazon's NoSQL database tool, SimpleDB and supporting several applications for both relational and non-relational databases as needed. It increases support for major and minor versions of the database system gradually and an admin can specify an engine version during the time of creating a database instance. Customers can spin up to six types of database engines within Amazon RDS including Amazon Aurora, PostgreSQL, MySQL, MariaDB, Oracle Database and SQL Server. By using AWS Database Migration Service, users can easily migrate or imitate their existing databases to Amazon RDS and can replicate to one-of-a-kind target database platforms. Multi-Availability Zone (AZ) allows users to automatically failover in different availability zones with synchronous data replication [20]. It does not provide shell access to DB cases

86   A. D. Antu et al.

and confines access to some system events and tables that need advanced privileges. It restricts 40 database instances per account and imposes additional restrictions for Oracle and SQL Server instances where a user only allowed up to 10 of each [21].

Amazon Aurora: Amazon Aurora is a MySQL and PostgreSQL-compatible relational database and migration from MySQL or PostgreSQL to Aurora is possible using standard import/export tools or snapshots. It offers a dispersed, fault-tolerant, self-restoration storage system that auto-scales up to 64 TB. Moreover, the applications, drivers, codes, and tools customers used to use in their existing databases are compatible with Amazon Aurora with little or no change. It provides excellent performance and accessibility with up to fifteen low latency read replicas, non-stop backup to Amazon S3 and replication across three AWS AZs. Amazon Aurora can process data up to five times faster than standard MySQL databases and three times faster than standard PostgreSQL databases [19]. It provides the safety, availability, and reliability of economic databases at 1/10th of the value.

Table 5. Comparison of Amazon RDS, Azure SQL database and Google cloud SQL.

Features	Relational database storage		
	Amazon RDS	Azure SQL database	Google cloud SQL
Service	Aurora, MySQL, MariaDB, Oracle, MS SQL Server, and PostgreSQL	Microsoft SQL Server	MySQL, PostgreSQL, or SQL server
Primary DBMS	Relational DBMS	Relational DBMS	Relational DBMS
Automatic software patching	Yes	Yes	Yes
Automatic scalability	Up to 64 TB	Not supported	Up to 30 TB
Data scheme	Yes	Yes	Yes
Typing	Yes	Yes	Yes
XML support	Yes	Yes	No
Secondary indexes	Yes	Yes	Yes
SQL support	Yes	Yes	Yes
APIs and connectivity	Amazon RDS API, query API	REST API	REST API, Cloud SQL Admin API
SQL server-side scripts	Transact SQL	Transact SQL	Transact SQL
Replication methods	Master-slave replication	Transactional replication	Master-slave replication
MapReduce	No	No	Yes

5.2 Azure SQL Database

Azure SQL Database is an intelligent, scalable, all-purpose fully managed cloud database service that gives the most important SQL Server engine compatibility and up to a 212% return on investment [22]. Migration to Azure SQL database is very easy from any existing or new version or application on Azure which can solve critical workloads for any enterprise or start-ups. Azure SQL Database enables the latest stable version of the Microsoft SQL Server database engine has two different purchasing models: a vCore-based purchasing model and a DTU-based purchasing model. The virtual core (vCore)-based purchasing model provides a choice between a monitored compute rank and a serverless compute rank. With monitored compute rank, the user can choose the number of computing resources that are continuously provisioned for their work. With the serverless compute rank, the user specifies the automatic scaling of the compute resources over a certain compute range. With this compute tier, the user can also automatically pause and resume their day-to-day activity. The vCore unit price per unit of time is lower than it is in the serverless compute tier. The database transaction unit (DTU)-based purchasing model offers a collection of compute and storage packages balanced for common workloads. Recently, users can run Azure Arc with Azure SQL according to their choice.

5.3 Google Cloud SQL

Google Cloud SQL is compatible with all basic applications and tools using MySQL, PostgreSQL, and SQL Server and provides automatic data backups, encryption, and ensuring greater than 99.95% availability worldwide using cloud infrastructure [23]. Cloud SQL supports private connectivity with Virtual Private Cloud (VPC) and connects a network firewall to control public network contact from user database instance. It offers automatically replicate the data to another zone and scale up the storage capacity when users are about to finish their limit. Therefore, automatic failover protects the database from any hardware or software failures and users do not have to spend time and money on storage capacity until they need it. Cloud SQL is easily connectable from App Engine, Compute Engine, Google Kubernetes Engine, and user workplace by using BigQuery to directly query in the Cloud SQL databases. Site Reliability Engineering (SRE) team provides 24/7 service for user support and migration from cloud SQL to MySQL databases or MySQL-compatible databases is possible with short downtime. In Table 5, a comparative evaluation of Relational Database Storage is exhibited.

6 No SQL Database

NoSQL stands for "not only SQL" and it can be considered as an alternate of RDB. Recently, NoSQL databases have become more popular as companies are moving cloud-based setup to supervise their databases and various applications to take advantage of faster and flexible data storage and recovery. It provides efficient schemes for building modern application development, functionality, reliability, low-cost and easy to use compare the traditional table structures found in relational databases. Numerous data models, including key-value, graph, document, in-memory, and search are using for retrieving and proper management. NoSQL can confine unstructured, structured data, semi-structured and polymorphic data and allow users a more simple, modern and controlled environment for their business with improved scalability.

6.1 Amazon DynamoDB/SimpleDB

Amazon DynamoDB and SimpleDB both are fully managed NoSQL database service that offers high scale, high-performance data storage, and recovery. The main difference of DynamoDB and SimpleDB are indexing their columns. DynamoDB indexes only primary key and SimpleDB indexes all the columns. This provides the DynamoDB much faster and delivers prompt service at any level of traffic request but less reliable than SimpleDB. To meet the customer request capacity with fast and consistent performance, DynamoDB can automatically distribute the data and traffic for the table over an adequate number of servers. Data items are stored on Solid State Drives (SSDs) and the service synchronously replicates data across three Availability Zones in all standard AWS regions to support built-in high availability and durability. In opposition, Amazon SimpleDB domain has limited storage up to 10 GB as well as limited request capacity, generally under 25 writes per second [25]. Besides, SimpleDB needs additional tables if customers need extra space and customers are also responsible to manage the segregating and re-partitioning of their data. DynamoDB supports primary indexes and several secondary indexes on documents and reads are consistent by default with a selection for strongly consistent reads where required. For SimpleDB, customers must pay for storing the amount of raw data every month. If one particular month, customers do not make and query or upload any new data then they will pay only for the data sitting there before. For DynamoDB, customers must pay for data they stored and servers query capacity hours every month [26].

6.2 Azure Table Storage

Azure Table storage is a structured non-relational database service in the cloud with key-value data types offered by Microsoft Azure. It has three versions with a schemeless design, and a table may have several units. Properties of an object are key-value pairs and the maximum number of key-value pairs an object can have is 256 [33]. Out of these 256 properties, three are mandatory properties. The first two mandatory properties are partition key and row key and each one of them is of type string. The partition key is used to partition the entities within the same table. Within a single partition, the row key must be unique, and a row key is used to identify a single object within the same partition. The timestamp is the third compulsory property that is produced by the system whenever an object is created or updated. An Azure table has a single index, and it is based first on the partition key and then on the row key. Thus, queries, where the partition key is mentioned, run faster compared to other queries where the partition key is not mentioned. There is no scope to create custom indexes like AppEngine's data store. Transactions are supported for entities in the same partition only. The user interface for accessing the table is via REST, LINQ and ADO.NET Data Services [27].

6.3 Google Datastore

An object in Google Datastore is known as an Entity and each entity has a set of properties that can have single or multiple values. The maximum size of an entity is 1 MB and each entity in datastore is uniquely identified by a key [33]. A set of entities that exist together in a kind of name and loosely kinds may be regarded as a table of the relational data model. A kind is a logical property that helps in classifying entities of different types. In most cases, an entity is identified by a combination of a kind and a unique ID. Each kind is replicated in three locations for reliability and the system supports strong consistency for operations across an entity group. The optimistic Concurrency Model is used for handling updates from multiple clients. The system allows users to create custom indexes of composite properties and the number of such indexes that can be created is limited to 100. For a query to execute, indexes must be built first and configured in the Google Datastore. There is no direct support for caching and if required applications must handle the same on their own. Datastore provides GQL, Google Query Language for queries and it has well-defined API for Python and Java [28].

6.4 Google Cloud Big Table

Google Cloud Bigtable is a No-SQL service option that can stretch to numerous rows and columns so that customers are able to store terabytes or up to petabytes of information. The single value in every row is indexed and known as the row key. Cloud Bigtable generally connects to the applications through numerous client libraries, with the additional support of the Apache HBase library for Java. Consequently, it adapts with the current Apache ecosystem of open-source Big Data software. It doesn't replicate data in different zones or regions that means it is faster and more efficient though it is less durable and available in the default configuration. Generally, it takes only a few minutes to balance the performance across all the nodes in the cluster under the load [29]. It needs to add a second cluster to the instance, and replication to replicate the data. In Table 6, the feature comparison of a few of the No SQL Database Storage provided by Amazon, Azure and Google Cloud has revealed.

Table 6. Comparison of Amazon DynamoDB, Amazon SimpleDB, Azure table storage, Google data store and Google cloud big table.

Features	No SQL database storage			
	Amazon DynamoDB/SimpleDB	Azure table storage	Google data store	Google cloud big table
Primary database model	Key-value store	Key-value store	Document and Key-value store	Distributed Key-value store
Server operating systems	Hosted	Hosted	Hosted	Hosted

(continued)

Table 6. (*continued*)

Features	No SQL database storage			
	Amazon DynamoDB/SimpleDB	Azure table storage	Google data store	Google cloud big table
Typing	Yes	Yes	Yes	No
Secondary indexes	Yes	No	Yes	No
APIs and other access methods	Dynamo-DB: Low-Level API, SimpleDB: REST API	REST API	REST APIs, JSON APIs	RPC data APIs, REST/HTTP APIs
SQL	No	No	SQL-like query language (GQL)	No
Division methods	None	Sharding	Sharding	Sharding
Map-Reduce	No	No	Yes	Yes
Max size of entity	400 KB	1 MB	1 MB	10 MB
Automatic data allocation	Dynamo-DB support, SimpleDB does not support	Support	Support	Support

7 Managed Data Warehouse

A data warehouse is a central source of information that customers can use to analyze their reports and managing data accurately to take critical decisions. It is a combination of multiple separate databases and accumulating all the data together the end-user can easily predict the primary information. Big companies and institutions allow data warehouse as the heart of the business information system with collecting data from all the business branches or units. Data warehouses mostly control the batch workloads that usually process a huge amount of bulk data and cut down the I/O for improving the performance per query. Nowadays, businesses can choose their compute and storage requirement as needed and this opportunity is saving them lots of money from over-distributing servers to control huge data supplies which are used only for short terms.

7.1 Amazon Redshift

Amazon Redshift offers a fully managed, petabyte-scale data warehouse service in the cloud. Customers can query open file systems including Parquet, ORC, JSON, Avro, CSV directly in S3 using traditional ANSI SQL. It provides the flexibility to store highly structured and frequently accessed data while also using structured, semi-structured, and unstructured data in S3. Transferring data from Redshift back to the user end enables data further analysis with AWS services like Amazon Athena, Amazon EMR, and Amazon SageMaker. With the anew merged query skill in Redshift, users can grasp into their operational, relational database. Natural integration with the AWS analytics ecosystem makes it easier to manage end-to-end data analytics without resistance. AWS Glue can be used for extracting and moving data into Redshift and Amazon Kinesis Data Firehose helps close real-time data analytics. Customers can also use Redshift to formulate their data to run machine learning systems with Amazon SageMaker [31].

Table 7. Comparison of Amazon Redshift, Azure SQL data warehouse and Google cloud big query.

Features	Managed data warehouse		
	Amazon Redshift	Azure synapse	Google cloud big query
Service	Petabyte sized cloud data warehouse	Limitless, large scale data warehouse	Controlling data repository with high demand public datasets
Database model	Enterprise-class relational DBMS	Enterprise-class relational DBMS	Enterprise-class relational DBMS
Max storage	64 TB	60 TB	10 GB free/month and up to 300 TB
Secondary indexes	Restricted	No	Yes
Partition method	Sharding	None	Sharding
XML support	No	No	No
Supported languages	All languages supporting JDBC/ODBC	.Net, Java, JavaScript, Objective-C, PHP, Python, Ruby	C#, Java, PHP
Transaction concepts	ACID	No	ACID
Server-side scripts	User defined function	User defined functions	Transact SQL
Foreign keys	Yes	No	Yes
MapReduce	No	No	Yes
Free trial	2 months	12 months	12 months

7.2 Azure Synapse

Azure Synapse is an analytics service that merges business data warehousing and Big Data analytics. Customers can choose either serverless on-demand or provisioned resources to query data. Analytics saves data in tables with columnar storage and mentions to the business bulk data warehousing features that are usually offered in Azure Synapse. This set-up remarkably reduces the data storage prices and advances the query capacity. Customers can run analytics on a gigantic scale when data is stored. With comparison with typical database systems, Synapse is fast and can process queries in seconds. This outcome can be used in global reporting applications or databases and business analysts realize the scenario and can take critical decisions for the future [32].

7.3 Google Cloud Big Query

Storing and querying Bulk datasets is time intense and costly without the proper hardware and infrastructure arrangements. BigQuery is a business data warehouse that solved this problem by allowing extremely fast SQL queries with the updated processing power of Google's infrastructure. Customers will only transfer their data into BigQuery, and it will manage the complexity. Also, customers can handle access permission to both the project and the data based on their business needs. It is a serverless and cost-effective cloud data warehouse solution that is developed to take quick business decisions. It is easy to set up and control and doesn't need a database manager. Gigabytes to petabytes data can be processed using ANSI SQL with zero operational cost. Proficiently operate analytics at scale with a 26%–34% lower three-year TCO than cloud data warehouse substitutes. In Table 7, a comparison of different characteristics of Managed Data Warehouse options, such as Amazon Redshift, Azure SQL Data Warehouse, and Google Cloud Big Query is demonstrated.

8   Conclusion

Our paper presents a direct comparison between the various services provided by Amazon AWS, Microsoft Azure, and Google Cloud Platform. By highlighting various features and by doing SWOT Analysis (Table 8, Table 9, Table 10) of these three providers, we have realized that the single "best" option depends on particular business needs. We conclude an enterprise must be diligent about thoroughly understanding its storage requirements and carefully weigh the strengths and weaknesses of various providers. Selecting a provider and a service is a significant decision with which a business must live, possibly for several years. Choosing the wrong solution can negatively a business's ability to adequately perform in the market.

Table 8. SWOT analysis AWS storage.

Strengths	Weaknesses
AWS launched in 2006 and right now Public cloud market share is 32.4% worldwide [30]	Difficult to use and overwhelming options
Dominant market position	Cost management
Extensive, mature applications	Database trends like NoSQL database
Support for large organizations	Free trial/testing options are limited
Extensive training	
Global reach	
Opportunities	Threats
More than $700 billion industry and offers immense potential Continued investment and expansions	Huge competitions with Microsoft Azure, google cloud, IBM
Companies are largely moving to the cloud because of the file storage variety it provides	Lack of knowledge of using application tools
A growing suite of products and services	Price war on services

Table 9. SWOT analysis Azure storage.

Strengths	Weaknesses
Azure launched in 2010 and public cloud market share is 17.6% worldwide [30]	Issues with documentation
Integration with Back-office IT applications	Incomplete management application tools
It supports .NET and other programming languages	Overexposed to pc market
Second largest provider	Lacking innovation
Integration with Microsoft tools and software	Lacking market leadership in Internet browser segment
Broad feature set	Azure Firewall is not secured enough
Hybrid cloud	
Support for open source	
Opportunities	Threats
One step expansion from enterprise space	Changing preferences of the consumers
Focusing more on hybrid cloud business	The opacity of engineers who don't use Microsoft heavy languages
Cost leadership strategy	Open-source projects

Table 10. SWOT analysis GCP storage.

Strengths	Weaknesses
Google Cloud launched in 2008 and public cloud market share is 6% worldwide [30]	Google massively relies on privacy, particularly it hides the information about algorithms
Google Network	Fewer services and poor customer-support
Commitment to open source and portability	A late participant to IaaS market
Incremental Billing	
Designed for cloud-native businesses	Historically not as business-focused
Deep discounts and flexible contracts with free trials	Overdependence on advertising
Instance flexibility	Compatibility reduction
DevOps expertise	
Secured infrastructure	
Environmental protection and Expendability	
Opportunities	Threats
Developers are interested in GCP as application data are available and easy to deploy	Lack of specific standard regulation (local, national and international)
Bring modern information solutions according to the last and new technology	The difficulty of migration from one to another platform
Good opportunity for making progress of SMEs without upfront investment	Long way to catch up as other services are offering huge opportunities
Adaptive to future needs and gradually improving on customer services	
Standardized process	

References

1. Fernández, V.: "SMiD Cloud Security", "Security In Data Cloud Storage" Whitepaper (2017). https://smidcloud.com/wpcontent/uploads/2017/07/Cloud_Storage_Security_Whitepaper-2017.pdf
2. RightScale 2019 State of the Cloud Report from Flexera. Flexera. https://www.flexera.com/about-us/press-center/rightscale-2019-state-of-the-cloud-report-from-flexera-identifies-cloud-adoption-trends.html. Accessed 28 Feb 2020
3. Cloud Storage Services – Amazon Web Services (AWS): Amazon Web Services, Inc. (2020). https://aws.amazon.com/products/storage/. Accessed 19 Feb 2020
4. Get highly secure cloud storage at massive scale with an Azure free account | Microsoft Azure: Azure.microsoft.com (2020). https://azure.microsoft.com/en-us/free/storage/. Accessed 13 Feb 2020
5. Cloud Storage: Object Storage | Google Cloud: Google Cloud (2020). https://cloud.google.com/storage. Accessed 10 Feb 2020

6. File storage, block storage, or object storage? Red Hat - We make open source technologies for the enterprise. https://www.redhat.com/en/topics/data-storage/file-block-object-storage. Accessed 29 Feb 2020
7. Kovacs, G.: Block Storage vs. Object Storage in the Cloud. Cloud.netapp.com (2020). https:// cloud.netapp.com/blog/block-storage-vs-object-storage-cloud. Accessed 25 Jan 2020
8. What is Cloud Object Storage? – AWS: Amazon Web Services, Inc. (2020). https://aws.ama zon.com/what-is-cloud-object-storage/. Accessed 25 Feb 2020
9. Cloud Object Storage | Store & Retrieve Data Anywhere | Amazon Simple Storage Service (S3). Amazon Web Services, Inc., (2020). https://aws.amazon.com/s3/. Accessed 25 Feb 2020
10. Object Storage Classes – Amazon S3: Amazon Web Services, Inc. (2020). https://aws.ama zon.com/s3/storage-classes/?nc=sn&loc=3. Accessed 20 Jan 2020
11. Docs.aws.amazon.com (2020). https://docs.aws.amazon.com/whitepapers/latestcost-optimi zation-storage-optimization/aws-storage-services.html. Accessed 21 Feb 2020
12. Introduction to Blob (object) storage - Azure Storage. Docs.microsoft.com (2020). https:// docs.microsoft.com/en-us/azure/storage/blobs/storage-blobs-introduction. Accessed 25 Feb 2020
13. Bucur, V., Dehelean, C., Miclea, L.: Object Storage in the Cloud and Multi-cloud: State of the Art and the research challenges. In: 2018 IEEE International Conference on Automation, Quality and Testing, Robotics (AQTR), pp. 1–6. IEEE, May 2018
14. Amazon Elastic Block Store (EBS) - Amazon Web Services. Amazon Web Services, Inc. (2020). https://aws.amazon.com/ebs/. Accessed 25 Feb 2020
15. Amazon Simple Queue Service (SQS) | Message Queuing for Messaging Applications | AWS. Amazon Web Services, Inc., (2020). https://aws.amazon.com/sqs/. Accessed 25 Feb 2020
16. Introduction to Azure Queues - Azure Storage. Docs.microsoft.com (2020). https://docs.mic rosoft.com/en-us/azure/storage/queues/storage-queues-introduction. Accessed 25 Feb 2020
17. Yoon, H., Gavrilovska, A., Schwan, K., Donahue, J.: Interactive use of cloud services: Amazon SQS and S3. In: 2012 12th IEEE/ACM International Symposium on Cluster, Cloud and Grid Computing (CCGrid 2012, pp. 523–530. IEEE, May 2012
18. Bruno Almeida, P.: Google Cloud Storage Options: Object, Block, and Shared File Stor age. Cloud.netapp.com (2020). https://cloud.netapp.com/blog/object-storage-block-and-sha red-file-storage-in-google-cloud. Accessed 25 Feb 2020
19. Amazon Aurora – Relational Database Built for the Cloud – AWS. Amazon Web Services, Inc. (2020). https://aws.amazon.com/rds/aurora/. Accessed 25 Feb 2020
20. Amazon RDS Frequently Asked Questions (FAQs) - Amazon Web Services (AWS). Amazon Web Services, Inc. (2020). https://aws.amazon.com/rds/faqs/. Accessed 25 Feb 2020
21. What is Amazon RDS (Relational Database Service)? - Definition from WhatIs.com. SearchAWS (2020). https://searchaws.techtarget.com/definition/Amazon-Relational-Dat abase-Service-RDS. Accessed 25 Feb 2020
22. SQL Database – Cloud Database as a Service | Microsoft Azure. Azure.microsoft.com (2020). https://azure.microsoft.com/en-us/services/sql-database/. Accessed 25 Feb 2020
23. Cloud SQL: Relational Database Service | Google Cloud. Google Cloud (2020). https://cloud. google.com/sql/. Accessed 25 Feb 2020
24. Cloud Pub/Sub | Google Cloud. Google Cloud (2020). https://cloud.google.com/pubsub/. Accessed 25 Feb 2020
25. Vogels, W.: Amazon DynamoDB – a fast and scalable NoSQL database service designed for internet scale applications. https://www.allthingsdistributed.com/2012/01/amazon-dyn amodb.html. Accessed 01 Mar 2020
26. FAQs: Amazon Web Services, Inc. (2020). https://aws.amazon.com/simpledb/faqs/. Accessed 11 Feb 2020

27. Introduction to Table storage - Object storage in Azure. Docs.microsoft.com (2020). https://docs.microsoft.com/bs-latn-ba/azure/storage/tables/table-storage-overview. Accessed 01 Feb 2020
28. Datastore Overview | Cloud Datastore Documentation | Google Cloud. Google Cloud (2020). https://cloud.google.com/datastore/docs/concepts/overview. Accessed 09 Jan 2020
29. Overview of Cloud Bigtable | Cloud Bigtable Documentation. Google Cloud (2020). https://cloud.google.com/bigtable/docs/overview. Accessed 09 Feb 2020
30. Canalys.com (2020). https://www.canalys.com/static/press_release/2020/Canalys---Cloud-market-share-Q4-2019-and-full-year-2019.pdf. Accessed 25 Feb 2020
31. Clark, S.: Redshift. Amazon (1997). https://aws.amazon.com/redshift/features/. Accessed 02 Mar 2020
32. What is Azure Synapse Analytics (formerly SQL DW)? - Azure SQL Data Warehouse. Docs.microsoft.com (2020). https://docs.microsoft.com/en-us/azure/sql-data-warehouse/sql-data-warehouse-overview-what-is. Accessed 02 Mar 2020
33. DB-Engines - Knowledge Base of Relational and NoSQL Database Management Systems. Db-engines.com (2020). https://db-engines.com/en/. Accessed 02 Mar 2020

COS2: Detecting Large-Scale COVID-19 Misinformation in Social Networks

Hailu Xu[1]([✉]), Macro Curci[1], Sophanna Ek[1], Pinchao Liu[3], Zhengxiong Li[2], and Shuai Xu[4]

[1] Department of Computer Engineering and Computer Science,
California State University, Long Beach, USA
hailu.xu@csulb.edu
[2] University of Colorado Denver, Denver, USA
zhengxiong.li@ucdenver.edu
[3] Facebook, Inc., Menlo Park, USA
pinchao@fb.com
[4] Case Western Reserve University, Cleveland, USA
sxx214@case.edu

Abstract. The ongoing COVID-19 pandemic is bringing an "infodemic" on social media. Simultaneously, the huge volume of misinformation (such as rumors, fake news, spam posts, etc.) is scattered in every corner of people's social life. Traditional misinformation detection methods typically focus on centralized offline processing, that is, they process pandemic-related social data by deploying the model in a single local server. However, such processing incurs extremely long latency when detecting social misinformation related to COVID-19, and cannot handle large-scale social misinformation. In this paper, we propose COS2, a distributed and scalable system that supports large-scale COVID-19-related social misinformation detection. COS2 is able to automatically deploy many groups to distribute deep learning models in scalable cloud servers, process large-scale COVID-19-related social data in various groups, and efficiently detect COVID-19-related tweets with low latency.

Keywords: COVID-19 infodemic · Social misinformation detection · Cloud computing

1 Introduction

The COVID-19 pandemic not only threatens human health, but also brings the "infodemic" of misinformation, e.g., fake news, social spam, and rumors, which seriously threatens the safety of the public's social life. The openness, flexibility, and high availability of social networks have accelerated the spread of misinformation during the COVID-19 pandemic. For example, misinformation widely spread in social networks has exacerbated the serious collapse of the world stock market, caused a sharp decline in the world economy, and disrupted government actions [4]. In general, identifying and preventing misinformation

K. Ye and L.-J. Zhang (Eds.): CLOUD 2021, LNCS 12989, pp. 97–104, 2022.
https://doi.org/10.1007/978-3-030-96326-2_7

of the "infodemic" in social networks poses huge challenges. It is difficult for ordinary people to determine whether the news or post is true or not based on their point of views. They can only wait for clarification from official media or experts, which usually takes a few days. However, even if the information is confirmed, fear, stress, and anxiety have spread widely to society.

Previous work has proposed various methods to identify COVID-19-related misinformation in social networks, but they usually focus on *small-scale local detection*, that is, (1) first, organize and process the limited data to a local machine; (2) then design and optimize the model offline; (3) finally, apply the model to local limited data [2,3,8,10]. However, this offline process is impractical for the current "infodemic": it only targets on a limited amount of social data, wastes a lot of time in offline deployment, and cannot instantly prevent the spread of pandemic-related misinformation. During the pandemic, there is an urgent need for a scalable platform that can quickly identify social misinformation related to the COVID-19 "infodemic".

In this paper, we propose a distributed system called COS2, which can support distributed deep learning models among many groups of cloud servers, and can efficiently and quickly detect social misinformation of COVID-19 at scale. The proposed design of COS2 consists of four major phases: first, it organizes the large-scale social data into many different groups according to topics, such as political-related, vaccine-related, and economic-related groups. This is suitable for the extremely large volume of pandemic-related social data streams that cannot be effectively handled by a single dataset. Second, each group consists of a master server and many worker servers to complete the detection task. COS2 supports data parallelism among groups, so that each server in a group has a copy of the model to process with a portion of the data. Third, each group can flexibly deploy its own distributed deep learning model (e.g., RNN, federated learning model) based upon the data it owns. Finally, online social network data can be processed in a timely manner by the distributed model to directly distinguish the misinformation. In addition, the misinformation detection process will be automatically completed in the distributed servers without manual intervention.

In the rest of the paper, we introduce the workflow and the functionality of COS2. We evaluate the system with preliminary social data in Google cloud servers. We believe that the flexibility of COS2 and its subsequent improvements in a scalable architecture can enable effective COVID-19 social misinformation detection in distributed cloud servers.

2 Design

2.1 Overview

COS2 is a distributed system that supports the detection of COVID-19 social misinformation from large-scale social network data. As shown in Fig. 1, the workflow in COS2 consists of four phases: (1) organizes large-scale social data into different groups; (2) creates the group structure that consists of a master

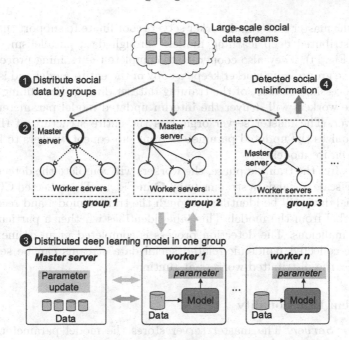

Fig. 1. The overview and workflow of COS2.

server and many worker servers; (3) deploys distributed deep learning models in the group; and (4) completes the COVID-19 related misinformation detection in an online fashion. Next, we introduce the details of each phase and discuss the functionalities of the system.

First, the huge volume of social data streams related to COVID-19 will be classified and organized into different groups via various topics or keywords (step ❶ in Fig. 1). In this phase, COS2 uses a script that can automatically normalize and pre-process the social data streams into formatted data. Next, it evaluates each post by using sentiment analysis tools and then identifies the post as a category. For example, based on the weights of the topic or keywords in the post, COS2 can separate the original posts into vaccine-related, political-related, or economic-related groups. Besides, it can categorize the original posts into figure-related or link-related groups via the characteristics of the content. Further, users can manually define the type of groups to provide more flexibility in further data analysis.

Second, COS2 deploys the groups in cloud servers and each group builds its own distributed deep learning models across the deployed servers, as shown in step ❷ in Fig. 1. In this step, each group is built on multiple servers, where it consists of a master server and many worker servers. The organization of the master and worker servers is flexible, depending on the size of the group and the deployment of the model. If one group is allocated to a large size of data, the number of worker servers is relatively large.

Third, the master server and worker servers coordinate to support the deployment of distributed deep learning models through data parallelism approach (step ❸ in Fig. 1)). They also cooperate to complete the training process of the model. In the group, each worker keeps a copy of the entire model and is responsible for processing a subset of the training dataset during the training process. Besides, the workers will deliver the interim updated model parameters to the master server. The master server organizes the entire structure of the group and synchronizes the updated parameters from subsequent workers to instantly update the entire model.

Finally, after the training phase, the workers will complete the detection process of large-scale social data streams (step ❹ in Fig. 1). The collected COVID-19 related social data will be identified through the trained model and receives the predicted label from the model. This label identifies whether a particular data instance is malicious. The detection process is completed in an online fashion, that is, the collected pandemic-related social data streams can be seamlessly processed by the distributed workers at runtime.

2.2   System Functionality

Parameter Server. The master server stores the model parameter to synchronize the model in the group. The model parameters (i.e., key-values) will be periodically synchronized after the worker servers send the interim parameters to the master when obtaining a new training dataset. Master averages the received parameters. Each worker will pull the updated weight vector from the parameter server and then update its own model with the new vector. Besides, it needs to push the updated weight vector back to the parameter server after updating the parameter vector.

Synchronization with Stragglers. The synchronization of the parameter is completed only after the master server aggregates the updated vectors from all the following workers. However, in some cases, one or several workers may encounter unpredicted dilemmas, such as network bandwidth limitation or downtime due to server failures (e.g., power cuts off). They will be the stragglers for the whole process. The synchronization will be greatly diminished by the straggler workers and it incurs extremely long latency when updating the global parameter.

In order to recover from stragglers, servers in the group will periodically exchange the live messages with others. COS2 sets a threshold for message communication and defines the strategy for recovering from stragglers. When a server fails to respond after a specific message communication period, it will be considered a straggler. The tasks previously assigned to the server will be transmitted to another active and free server. The relevant parameter of the straggler will be recalculated in the new server and the group will re-synchronize the global parameters.

Fault Tolerant of Parameters. Parameter synchronization is the key point for achieving efficient social misinformation detection. Fail to update or loss

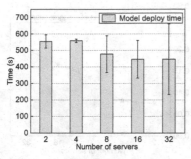

(a) Time of model deployment.

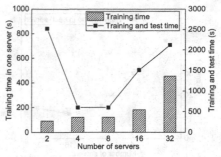

(b) Time of training and test.

Fig. 2. Results in COS2. (a) shows the model deployment time in the system. (b) shows the training and test time in the detection.

of parameters will result in the failure of the entire model training, thereby destroying the overall performance of large-scale social data processing. When the volume of parameters in each group is relatively small, the parameter server can instantly save the parameters (e.g., key-value pairs) in the local memory or storage. In some cases, the temporary parameters will be very large, such as millions or billions of values, a single parameter server may not be sufficient to manage such large parameters due to the network bandwidth bottleneck for parameter delivery and limited storage capacity. In this case, COS2 separately saves the parameters into different servers within the group. And many servers coordinate the updating and saving of parameters.

In addition, COS2 provides a parameter management structure to ensure the availability and robustness of the interim parameters. Due to server failure or bandwidth bottleneck, interim parameters from workers and parameters saved in the master server or groups may be lost. To solve this problem, COS2 creates a replica of parameters in each server so that the replica of parameters can be used to restore the lost or damaged parameters. The replica will be saved across the distributed servers in the group.

3 Evaluations

We evaluate COS2 by deploying several masters and workers on the Google Cloud AI Platform. The evaluation is built on 32 n1-standard-4 machine instances within the Google Cloud. Each instance includes 4 vCPUs, 15 GBs of memory, 128 GBs persistent disks, and 2 Gbps of bandwidth.

The training dataset consists of 10,000 tweets with labels of 1 (spam) or 0 (non-spam). The test dataset is the collected social stream data around 500,000 instances. We implement a Keras word embedding tokenizer to process the raw tweets into encoded vectors of length 100. We also add several flags for specific keywords or url links that are associated with spam. The training data consists of 104 columns (a column for each encoded word in the 100 length vector and

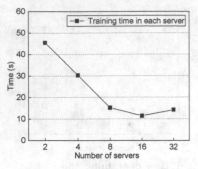

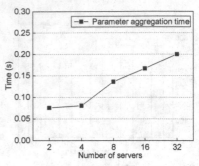

(a) Average training time in one server.   (b) Parameter aggregation time.

Fig. 3. (a) shows the model average training time in each server. (b) shows the time of aggregating all parameters in one group.

Table 1. Preliminary results of spam classification.

Model	F1 score	Precision	Recall
COS2	64%	64%	71%

4 columns for specific keywords and links). Around 14% of the collected tweets are classified as spam.

The deployed model is a fully connected deep learning model consisting of 4 layers and is developed in Tensorflow with Keras [1]. The input layer includes 100 neurons with a relu activation function, the second layer consists of 200 neurons with a relu activation function, the third layer includes 10 neurons and a relu activation function, and finally the output layer includes 1 output with a sigmoid activation function.

We first evaluate the deployment time of models in workers of one group. The deployment time is the time between submitting distributed jobs to the worker that is ready for the training. Figure 2a shows that the average of deployment time is around 554 s regardless of the number of workers. It is consistent with the increment of workers in the system. Figure 2b shows the training and test time in the servers. The raw training time linearly increases with the increment of workers, such as 2 workers with a training time of 91 s, 32 workers have around 454 s. Figure 3a shows when increasing the workers, the average training time of each server can be reduced, which indicates the potential effectiveness of scalability in handling large-scale social data. But when workers in one group become larger, the training time will increase due to the overhead of managing parameters with a larger pool of machines and parameters, as shown in Fig. 3b. It indicates that when deploying the large-scale social data in many groups, an appropriate control group size should be a good choice for efficient processing. Besides, as shown in Table 1, the detection performance from the model shows that our model achieves around 64% in F1 score with 64% in precision and 71% in recall. In the future, we will thoroughly evaluate the system from the scalability and optimize the performance of models with comparing other state-of-the-art methods.

4   Related Work

Many previous studies had focused on analyzing misinformation from online social networks [2,5–7,11–15]. For example, Ceinllis et al. [2] analyzed the information spreading models in the COVID-19 related social data from five different platforms, where they found that the interaction patterns and the peculiarity of the users are key roles in the misinformation spreading. Yang et al. [14] proposed that low-credibility information spreads via retweets and social bots are deeply involved into the spreading of misinformation. Wang et al. [7] investigated the COVID-19 related health beliefs on Twitter, where they showed that the number of users tweeting was amplifying in an epidemic manner and partially intensify the infodemic. Zhang et al. [15] analyzed the social posts related to the COVID-19 misinformation on major China social platforms, and they found that the infodemic shows gradual progress, videoization, and repeated fluctuations. Germani and Biller-Andorno [5] investigated the anti-vaccination posts on Twitter and showed that the anti-vaccination supporters provide strong influences in the local community and only a small fraction of profiles can strongly influence the global social media. Sharma et al. [9] investigated the misleading contents on Twitter and analyzed the spreading patterns of prominent tweets, patterns in different countries and trends. Islam et al. [6] analyzed the role of motivation factors and personal attributes in the spreading of misinformation of infodemic, and they found social users who suffer from deficient self-regulation are more likely to share the misinformation.

5   Conclusion

In this paper, we propose COS2, a distributed and scalable system that supports large-scale COVID-19-related social misinformation detection. By automatically deploying many flexible groups with distributed deep learning models in scalable cloud servers, COS2 can quickly process the large-scale social data streams and detect the social misinformation related to COVID-19 "infodemic" from social data streams.

In the future, we will focus on the design of system infrastructure, explore the scalability of the implementation on cloud, improve the automatic deployment of models, achieve robust fault tolerance in terms of parameter loss, and ensure fast recovery from stragglers. Moreover, we plan to investigate the various characteristics of social content so that to optimize the runtime performance of misinformation detection. Finally, we will extend COS2 to large-scale cloud servers and evaluate it with vast social networks related applications.

References

1. Keras & Tensorflow 2 (2021). https://keras.io/guides/
2. Cinelli, M., et al.: The covid-19 social media infodemic. Sci. Rep. **10**(1), 1–10 (2020)
3. Ding, K., Shu, K., Li, Y., Bhattacharjee, A., Liu, H.: Challenges in combating covid-19 infodemic-data, tools, and ethics. arXiv preprint arXiv:2005.13691 (2020)
4. Elhadad, M.K., Li, K.F., Gebali, F.: Detecting misleading information on Covid-19. IEEE Access **8**, 165201–165215 (2020)
5. Germani, F., Biller-Andorno, N.: The anti-vaccination infodemic on social media: a behavioral analysis. PLoS ONE **16**(3), e0247642 (2021)
6. Islam, A.N., Laato, S., Talukder, S., Sutinen, E.: Misinformation sharing and social media fatigue during covid-19: an affordance and cognitive load perspective. Technol. Forecast. Soc. Change **159**, 120201 (2020)
7. Luo, Y.: Using tweets to understand how covid-19-related health beliefs are affected in the age of social media: Twitter data analysis study. J. Med. Internet Res. **23**(2), e26302 (2021)
8. Shahi, G.K., Dirkson, A., Majchrzak, T.A.: An exploratory study of covid-19 misinformation on twitter. Online Soc. Netw. Media **22**, 100104 (2021)
9. Sharma, K., Seo, S., Meng, C., Rambhatla, S., Liu, Y.: Covid-19 on social media: analyzing misinformation in twitter conversations. arXiv preprint arXiv:2003.12309 (2020)
10. Wu, Y., Fang, Y., Shang, S., Jin, J., Wei, L., Wang, H.: A novel framework for detecting social bots with deep neural networks and active learning. Knowl.-Based Syst. **211**, 106525 (2021)
11. Xu, H., Guan, B., Liu, P., Escudero, W., Hu, L.: Harnessing the nature of spam in scalable online social spam detection. In: 2018 IEEE International Conference on Big Data (Big Data), pp. 3733–3736. IEEE (2018)
12. Xu, H., Hu, L., Liu, P., Guan, B.: Exploiting the spam correlations in scalable online social spam detection. In: Da Silva, D., Wang, Q., Zhang, L.-J. (eds.) CLOUD 2019. LNCS, vol. 11513, pp. 146–160. Springer, Cham (2019). https://doi.org/10.1007/978-3-030-23502-4_11
13. Xu, H., et al.: Oases: an online scalable spam detection system for social networks. In: 2018 IEEE 11th International Conference on Cloud Computing (CLOUD), pp. 98–105. IEEE (2018)
14. Yang, K.C., Torres-Lugo, C., Menczer, F.: Prevalence of low-credibility information on twitter during the covid-19 outbreak. arXiv preprint arXiv:2004.14484 (2020)
15. Zhang, S., Pian, W., Ma, F., Ni, Z., Liu, Y.: Characterizing the covid-19 infodemic on Chinese social media: exploratory study. JMIR Public Health Surveill. **7**(2), e26090 (2021)

Author Index

Printed in the United States
by Baker & Taylor Publisher Services

Printed in the United States
by Baker & Taylor Publisher Services